Finding Hope...
In a Hurried World

▶ A Fast Read to Serenity and Meaningful Living ◀

G.A. Warren

Copyright © 2017 by G. A. Warren

Unless otherwise noted all Scripture taken from the
New King James Version ®.
Copyright ©1982 by Thomas Nelson, Inc.
Used by Permission. All rights reserved.

Scripture quotations taken from the Amplified Bible,
Copyright © 1954, 1958, 1962, 1964, 1965, 1987
By the Lockman Foundation
Used by permission

Scripture taken from the New American Standard Bible,
© 1960, 1962, 1963, 1968, 1971, 1972, 1973, 1975, 1977, 1995
by the Lockman Foundation, Used by permission.

Quoted passages by Charles H. Spurgeon from
Spurgeon's Expository Encyclopedia.
Reprinted 1984 by Baker Book House
Used by permission

Scripture references cited by C.H. Spurgeon
from the Authorized King James Version

All rights reserved. No part of this publication may be reproduced, photocopied, stored in a retrieval system or transmitted in any form or by any means—whether, electronic, photocopy, audio recording, or by future invention without the prior written permission of the publisher.

ISBN-10: 1544941234
ISBN-13: 978-1544941233

G.A. Warren Books, International
North Scituate, Rhode Island • gawarrenbooks.com

Printed in United States of America

* * *

Dedicated to those madly
racing down life's highway
watching hope disappear
in the mirror.

Contents

Introduction iii

PART 1: GAINING INSIGHT

Something is Missing 1
Getting Nowhere Fast 9
Keeping Up with the Joneses 13
What's the Rush? 19
Seeing Things as They Really Are 29
When Monkeys Run Wild 41

PART 2: FINDING DIRECTION

Discovering Living Hope 51
Defining Hope 63
The Truth Behind Living Hope 83
What Science Has to Say 93
A Quick Study on Hope 99
Personal Glimpses #1 109
Personal Glimpses #2 113
Waitin' for the Chewing Gum 117
The Poetry of Hope 122
Final Words of Hopeful Men 125
Three Key Truths to Living Hope 129
A God of Love 157
Acknowledgments 164

Introduction

The idea for *Finding Hope...in a Hurried World* was born in the rush of Boston's Logan Airport. While searching the terminal newsstand for something to read I ran across Time magazine. Splashed across its cover was a headline defining a culture driven to extremes:

"The Rat Race!
How America Is Running Itself Ragged."

There's little need for magazines to tell us we're "running...ragged." Our lives are evidently spinning at historic speeds. Like a laser beam we shoot into each new day focused—driven—rushed.

A boarding announcement erupted overhead as I thumbed through the magazine. The pace around me jumped into high gear as travelers focused on reaching their departure gates. I stuffed the magazine under my arm and worked my way to the cashier. In the rush of the moment I hit on an idea. What better way to get the message of real hope out to time-pressed people than in a quick read someone might snatch at a bookstand or checkout line? Reader's Digest has successfully used this philosophy of a condensed read for decades. I determined to jot down some helpful thoughts to point those losing hope in the midst their hectic lives in the right direction.

Finding Hope…in a Hurried World is intended to be a grab-and-go, fast read, comprised of short chapters peppered with quips, quotes, and anecdotes. Perfect for those on the run.

Two goals were kept in mind while writing this book. First, to assure the reader that a living hope is available to everyone—no matter where they are in life. And secondly, to encourage readers to personally take hold of this hope in the midst of their stress-filled, and at times, hurtful lives. On the following pages you'll find practical truths and applications, along with the views and testimonies of others who, perhaps like yourself, vitally needed unfailing hope. I trust you will find just what your life has needed all along: *Hope…in a Hurried World.*

— G.A. Warren

Part 1
Gaining Insight

In all things it is *better* to hope than despair.

~ Johann Goethe ~

Something is Missing

Humans are strange creatures. We run faster when we lose our way. Instead of pausing to regroup, we ricochet from place to place. Three words describe our times: hurry, worry, and bury.
— Charles R. Swindoll
Three Steps Forward Two Steps Back

Logan Airport is a blur of activity. Travelers scramble for departure gates as new arrivals pour down escalators to retrieve their luggage before hitting Boston's heavy traffic. A boarding announcement reverberates down the concourse accelerating the already frenzied pace around me.

Reaching my gate I sense the mounting impatience among fellow passengers as our own departure time approaches. From behind the kiosk an airline attendant announces permission to board our flight. A line instantly materializes and anxiously inches forward as boarding passes are processed.

A similar scene unfolds upon our arrival. A flight attendant announces debarkation and like lemmings we spill into an all-too-narrow aisle. In the crush of the moment I question why sensible adults are so eager to crowd into yet another line only to wait while forward passengers grab their carry-ons and exit the plane. The answer is obvious—we're all in a hurry.

We live in a rushed and chaotic world. And while airport rituals can be humorous at times with their hurry-up-and-wait syndrome, the unrelenting pace of modern life has shattered the hope for many of ever finding much needed relief from their daily pressures.

Today's assumption is that overstuffed schedules and goal-driven activities will deliver what we desire most out of life: a sense of significance, inner peace, and meaningful living—the very qualities that comprise a full and happy life.

Seven hundred years ago Thomas Aquinas keenly observed, "There is within every soul a thirst for happiness and meaning." This is no less true today then when Aquinas first made his observation. Yet growing numbers are forced to admit the dizzying pace of modern life has failed to deliver on these prized goals. Some feel they may never brush the face of true happiness or find real meaning to life. They sense that perhaps Thoreau was right all along, "The mass of men live lives of quiet desperation."

Far from being full, we find our lives running on empty. Something is desperately wrong. That sense that life has not quenched our "thirst for happiness and meaning" awkwardly persists. This unsettled feeling is all too common regardless of social status, degree of wealth, or for those fortunate few who have achieved the "dream of a lifetime." In an effort to overcome our frustrations we strive for yet greater achievements or reach for still higher goals. With our lives spinning nearly out of control our hope is misguided by the notion that the abundant life is somehow tied to running faster, stuffing our schedules full, and buying more things. Trapped in the fast lane of our own making, we mistakenly look for answers in all the wrong places. As one day blurs into the next we find ourselves desperately seeking an exit off the highway of hurry in search of answers—and much needed relief.

LOSING THE DREAM

Singing sensation Susan Boyle exploded onto the world stage in 2009. She gained instant notoriety with her dynamic rendition of *I Dreamed a Dream* on the reality show "Britain's Got Talent." Her amazing vocals immediately captured the world's attention. Within 24 hours of the program's airing, over a million viewers from around the globe watched her performance on *You Tube*. To date, viewers of that original performance now number well over 200 million. Her debut album was so anticipated it topped Amazon's bestseller list nearly three months before its release. Within six weeks of its release the album went multi-platinum and sold over three million copies. *I Dreamed a Dream* became Susan Boyle's signature song. Ironically her dream of becoming a celebrated singer became a reality by means of a song about a woman who lost her dream. The closing lines of the song reflect what life cruelly stole from this woman—her dream—her hope.

> *I had a dream my life would be,*
> *So different from this hell I'm living;*
> *So different now from what it seemed,*
> *Now life has killed the dream I dreamed.*

The lyrics are sobering, yet they express a common sentiment shared by many. Little has turned out as they once hoped. Their dreams lay dashed upon the rocky shoals of turmoil and disappointment. For them, and perhaps for you, hope has all but vanished.

SEARCHING FOR MEANING

George was a hard worker, but soon became disillusioned with the business world. In an act of desperation, he quit his job and determined to find the meaning of life. After several months of searching for answers he learned of a lama who spent his entire life on a mountaintop in Tibet. George was convinced that if he could speak with this man he would find his answer. Hopeful, George sold everything he owned and flew to Tibet. He hired a guide to bring him to the lama's mountain. After hiking for hours they reached the base of the mountain. The guide explained to George that a seeker of life's meaning must make the final leg of the journey alone. Undaunted, George climbed for days. He rationed his food, eating only enough to keep himself going. Finally, with strength nearly gone, he reached the mountain's summit. There in the distance sat the lama.

George approached the holy man. Standing before him, he bowed and said, "Sir, I have sacrificed everything and risked my life to reach you. I have been searching for the meaning of life and I believe you are the only one who can provide the answer."

The lama sat quietly for a few moments. Then, in a soft, melodic tone he murmured, "Life is like a river."

George waited, but the lama remained silent.

With patience exhausted George blurted out, "What do you mean, 'Life is like a river?' I sacrificed everything to find the meaning of life and all you can say is, 'Life is like a river?'"

The lama shrugged, "Okay," he said, "life is *not* like a river."

Poor George. For all his troubles he never found his answer. Like George, we intuitively sense life has some deeper meaning; some greater reason beyond the daily rush for accomplishment.

We tend to hinge life's meaning to goals, interests, or responsibilities; whether it's climbing the corporate ladder, chauffeuring children to soccer practice, or starting up a new business. Ask any parent concerning life's purpose and you'll hear about raising children and caring for the family. Question a career-minded employee and you'll hear a detailed plan for moving up the corporate ladder and building a larger home. A few souls may be honest enough to confess they find there's little more to life than making money. Others find hobbies, playing sports, or adding items to a lifelong collection provide a sense of purpose. Such endeavors hold a special significance, yet we can't escape the notion that there has to be something more to life than the endless rush of our pursuits—no matter how noble the cause; how pure the motive; or how important the task.

> "I thought it was very peculiar that I had acquired everything I had wanted as a child—wealth, fame and accomplishment in my career. I had beautiful children and a lifestyle that seemed terrific, and yet I was totally and miserably unhappy. I found it very frightening that one could acquire all these things and still be so miserable." —Rachel Welch, *Actress*

Naturally life's objectives are important to us, they offer a purpose in life. But they don't answer the nagging question; is there a rationale for these objectives? In other words, while we see these purposes in life, we're left wondering if there is some meaning behind it all.

TIME TO REEVALUATE

Ernő Rubik, famed inventor of the Rubik's cube, may have hit the nail on the head when he said, "Our whole life is solving puzzles."

Jigsaw puzzles are a favorite pastime for many. For the avid enthusiast the final reward is when that last piece is snapped into place. Yet how disappointing when, after spending countless hours on a formidable 1,000-piece puzzle, that last piece turns out to be missing. All hope of finishing the puzzle is gone. The colorful image clearly  matches the box top photo but our eye is irresistibly drawn to that single missing piece.

Life is like that. We easily identify the "box top" photo of our responsibilities and accomplishments, but we're aware something remains missing. There's a sense that life has somehow held out on us; that it owes us something more for all our efforts.

Some of us are painfully aware that what once inspired us has lost its luster. Those purposes tied to our responsibilities have become dry to the palate. What once held great meaning for us has lost its significance. We've become emotionally detached from our regular routine. In truth we're simply going through the motions. Emotionally, we're running on empty, often falling prey to discouragement or disillusionment.

Without remorse the rat race wears us down both physically and emotionally. Yet relentlessly it compels us to keep pace with its frenzied hurry.

Living at warp-speed we are weary to the bone. We long for rest in a restless world. Some of us are wondering if it's reasonable to believe that slowing down would help us find peace and contentment and life's deeper meaning.

Obsessively checking our smartphones, day planners, or calendars for what's next, I suspect secretly many of us want to carve out a large block of time all for ourselves. At the very least we long to pull off the highway of hurry before tomorrow's frenzy kicks in again. But instead, we keep in the fray, telling ourselves that just around the next bend we'll find that missing piece of the puzzle—it's only a matter of time.

In the midst of life's pursuits questions begin to surface. Is there more to life than just earning a living and paying a mortgage? Is disappointment something I have to live with? Why do I feel unfulfilled in life? Are the sacrifices I make worth all my efforts? Does my life possess genuine significance?

Answers to these questions, or others, won't be found by running ourselves ragged. Our sensibilities tell us if there are valid answers—if there is real hope in finding that missing piece of the puzzle—it must be tied to something more secure than our constantly changing world. It must be tied to something more reasonable than the empty promises of the never-ending rat race. 📖

Getting Nowhere Fast

> "It takes all the running you can do,
> to keep in the same place."
> —The Red Queen
> *Through the Looking Glass*, Lewis Carroll

In his twenties George Frideric Handel (1685-1759) had already established a reputation throughout Europe as an outstanding organist. By the time he entered his thirties Handel had became a successful composer. After moving to London, he decided to build his reputation as a composer and continued writing music for the next two decades. He primarily wrote operas for the upper class.

The problem Handel faced was that by the time he wrote an opera, rehearsed it, and performed it for his audience he was deep in debt. His income from each opera went to paying the debts he incurred during composing and rehearsing. It took about two months to ready an opera that would run for only three or six nights. A well-received opera might run up to eleven nights. Having then paid his bills, Handel immediately started on the next opera.

For twenty years his life became a frantic cycle of churning out more and more operas to pay his debts. He lived on the edge of debtor's prison day in and day out. Sound vaguely familiar? It should. Millions live hand-to-mouth, paycheck-to-paycheck in the hopes of keeping the hounds of debt's consequences at bay. The Red Queen was right, "It takes all the running you can do, to keep in the same place."

At some point reality finally hits—escape is impossible. We are trapped in the fevered-pace of personal obligations, production schedules, mandated deadlines, or a rash of clients all clamoring for delivery, "Yesterday!" The relentless pace of modern life affects everyone whether urbanite, suburbanite, or Midwestern farmer. And the rat race shows no signs of slowing. On the contrary, the whirlwind of life's incessant activities is spinning faster and faster with each passing year.

The maelstrom of contemporary living is more demanding for working women. Their rush doesn't end when the front door opens after a hard day's work. Now comes managing home and family, adding to the stress of an already busy schedule. The frenzied pace never slows.

Besides family to care for and homes to run, there's shopping to finish, volunteer meetings to attended, elderly parents to tend, children to chauffeur, career concerns to fulfill—need I go on? And while these responsibilities may not reflect every woman's lifestyle, others have their own exhaustive "must-do" lists, responsibilities, meetings, and household chores to accomplish before pillowing their heads at night. Ironically, in an age of limitless time saving devices, women seem to have less time than ever to—dare I say it—smell the roses. Their schedules are packed to overflowing and life is bursting out at the seams.

VACATION SITUATION

In a desperate attempt for relief we rearrange, reshuffle, and reorganize our schedules to squeeze in some downtime for a much-needed vacation. If your vacations are anything like mine they're mostly spent hustling from one tourist attraction to the next. They're anything but relaxing. Sightseeing, daily excursions, whirlwind tours, and airports all leave us exhausted rather than refreshed. Worse yet, we insist on "staying in touch" while away. Instead of enjoying the resort's sun and surf we're surfing the Internet, shooting emails to the office, or texting incessantly. With an expectation of returning home well refreshed and fully relaxed, the reality turns out quite the opposite. We're back home painfully aware we need another vacation to recover from the first one.

In today's hurried world some much-needed rest and relaxation seems to be as elusive as the proverbial pot-of-gold at the end of the rainbow. Our vocabulary has suddenly expanded to include such terms as "burn out," "stress-related illness," "emotional overload," or "occupational exhaustion." More troubling is that lately these terms tend to be in the forefront of our thinking. At the end of the day, many of us will climb into bed, pillow our heads, and ask ourselves, "Is this it? Is this what life is all about?"

Suddenly we feel like that pet hamster running incessantly on its exercise wheel—and getting nowhere fast. For all our efforts, we yearn to know only one thing: Is there hope for serenity in a world spinning madly out of control?

Though a work of fiction, Charles Dickens borders on the prophetic in describing the present mood of our nation in his opening lines from *A Tale of Two Cities*:

> It was the best of times, it was the worst of times, it was the age of wisdom, it was the age of foolishness, it was the epoch of belief, it was the epoch of incredulity, it was the season of hope, it was the winter of despair, we had everything before us, we had nothing before us, we were all going direct to Heaven, we were all going direct the other way—in short, the period was so far like the present period...

In every generation, life has been a mixture of good and bad, pain and peace, happiness and sorrow. It's no different today. But no matter how crazy our lives get, our "winter of despair" can be turned into a "season of hope." 📖

Keeping Up with the Joneses

> "We are impoverishing ourselves in pursuit of a consumption goal that is inherently unachievable."
> —*The Overspent* American, Juliet Schor

The comic strip "Keeping up with the Joneses" by Arthur R. ("Pop") Morand ran in many newspapers from 1914 to 1958. It chronicled the artist's humorous experiences of living in the newly emerging suburbs of the early twentieth century. Fast-forward a century and many lives are anything but humorous. For some Americans the dream has lately become little more than a financial nightmare as they scramble to satisfy their insatiable appetite for more.

In typical modern fashion much of the blame for financial woes are placed on either the economy or the government. Yet the root of the problem is often much closer to home. The culprit turns out to be our yearning to "keep up with the Joneses." Take for instance the 2006 "Necessity or Luxury" survey conducted by the Pew Research Center. They found nearly 33% of Americans now view cable or satellite TV as a necessity, up from 17% in

1996. The poll went on to reveal that now 51% of us can't live without a computer, up from 26% in 1996. Some items that were seen as an extravagance (or didn't exist in 1996) have also jumped onto the "necessity list" by a growing percentage of Americans:

- Cell Phones: 49%
- Flat-screen TV: 5%
- High-speed Internet: 29%
- IPod: 3%

You can be certain these percentages have increased significantly over the years.

What is now termed "conspicuous consumption," that is, the pursuit of happiness through consumerism has resulted in emotional distress and economic hardship for exploding numbers of Americans. Add to this, record-high unemployment, rising retail prices, along with skyrocketing health insurance and college costs and we have awakened from the American dream to face a harsh reality. A majority of households now work two or more jobs. Yet they are barely, if at all, able to make ends meet. Despite heroic efforts to keep heads above water many are drowning in a sea of debt.

Financial battles are being lost on every front. Home foreclosures remain high and the full-time job market remains tight. It's not unusual for companies to receive hundreds, if not thousands, of online résumés when advertising a job opening. The hope for a brighter future has been severely tarnished by economic uncertainty. Household goals for financial freedom are being squeezed lifeless by an all-too-tight budget month after month. The hope of becoming debt free grows smaller with each credit card payment and unexpected repair bill. For those unable to find work, the outlook is bleaker still.

Frustration, anxiety, and stress are now uninvited guests in our efforts to reach the elusive dream. In an attempt to "keep up with the Joneses" we are beset by both financial and emotional pressure. As one TV commercial points out, "Life comes at you fast." How true! So does mounting debt when facing unemployment or paychecks unable to keep up with rising prices; or, in the case of trying to "keep up with the Joneses," uncontrolled spending. The cruel reality for some is their goal of finally "arriving" remains just out of reach.

Somebody humorously observed, "We try to keep up with the Joneses, but when we finally catch up with them—*they refinance!*" Fortunately, an answer to our rush for more is close at hand. It's gaining an understanding that life has a broader and deeper meaning than simply capturing the American dream.

MONEY MATTERS

Benjamin Franklin was a man of remarkable abilities. Aside from being a distinguished inventor and innovator he was also a man of noble character and unusual insight. His acute capacity to understand the spirit of his time led to his support of the American Revolution followed by a long career as an outstanding statesmanship on behalf of the new Republic. In addition to his many accomplishments, Franklin published *Poor Richard's Almanack*. The periodical appeared from 1732 to 1758 and became a best seller in the American colonies. While Franklin's publication carried information typical for an almanac, it is chiefly remembered for its many pithy sayings. A number of which are still around today. Many of his maxims counseled for thrift as in, "A penny saved is a penny earned." Or his warning against foolish spending with, "Beware of little expenses, a small leak will sink a great ship." And it was Franklin who wisely observed,

> Money has never made a man happy, yet, nor will it. There is nothing in its nature to produce happiness. The more a man has, the more he wants. Instead of its filling a vacuum, it makes one. If it satisfies one want, it doubles and trebles that want another way. That was a true proverb of the wise man, rely upon it: "Better is little with the fear of the Lord, than great treasure, and trouble therewith."

Modern culture has adopted the misguided notion that money is the basis for happiness. We have come to believe that in some mystical way wealth adds value to life. For those trapped in the rat race of financial gain, or crushed under the social pressure to advance, or trudging off to a few more hours overtime on a job that could soon evaporate, the expression "life with meaning" seems a paradox to the never-ending cycle to acquire more or to simply make ends meet.

With some much-needed humor for our sullen age "Ready to Retire" reflects the fallacy of supposing money is what really matters:

> He always said he would retire,
> When he had made a million clear.
> And so he toiled into the dusk,
> From day to day, from year to year!
>
> At last he put his ledgers up,
> And laid his stock reports aside.
> And when he started out to live,
> He found he had already died!

A hope for happiness that depends solely on money will utterly fail when facing circumstances beyond its buying power or influence. Money cannot cure the terminally ill; neither can it mend broken relationships. It cannot buy love or true friendship. It altogether fails in bringing substantive meaning to life. For this reason alone money fails as a basis for genuine hope.

> For this reason alone money fails as the basis for genuine hope.

In our hurried and hectic world fortunes can be lost, savings accounts depleted, 401K plans laid waste, and houses mortgaged a second and third time. The changing face of industry and business, with its focus on global commerce, has eliminated countless thousands of American jobs, adversely affecting millions of lives. Yet, in light of this reality comes this bit of encouragement:

Don't Be Discouraged!

If a man loses his property at thirty or forty years of age, it is only a sharp discipline generally, by which later he comes to large success. It is all folly for a man or woman to sit down in mid-life discouraged. The marshals of Napoleon came to their commander and said, "We have lost the battle and we are being cut to pieces." Napoleon took his watch from his pocket, and said, "It is only two o'clock in the afternoon. You have lost the battle, but we have time to win another. Charge upon the foe!" Let our readers who have been defeated thus far in the battle of life not give up in despair. With energy and God's blessing they may yet win a glorious victory.

—*Anonymous*

Hope is like the sun, which, as
we journey toward it, casts the
shadow of our burden behind us.

~ *Samuel Smiles (1812-1904)* ~

What's the Rush?

> "A kitten is chiefly remarkable for rushing about like mad at nothing whatever, and generally stopping before it gets there."
> — Agnes Repplier

One New Yorker prided himself on his reputation for punctuality. The secret of his success lay in his disciplined routine. Typically his alarm went off at 6:30A.M. With great efficiency he would quickly shower, shave, eat his breakfast, brush his teeth, gather up his briefcase, get into his car, drive to the Staten Island ferry, park his car, ride the ferry to downtown Manhattan, disembark, walk briskly to his office building, ride the elevator to the seventeenth floor, hang up his coat, open his briefcase, spread his papers out on his desk, and sit down to work at precisely 8:00A.M.

For years this man's routine never varied. But one morning his alarm failed to go off and he overslept fifteen minutes. When he finally woke up he was panic-stricken. He rushed through his shower, hastily ran the razor across his face, skipped breakfast, quickly brushed his teeth, snatched his briefcase, jumped into his car, sped to the ferry, parked, and bolted out of his car just in time to see the ferry out on the water several feet from the dock. He assured himself he could make it and ran down the dock toward the ship at full speed. Reaching the edge of the pier he gave an enormous leap out over the water and miraculously landed on the deck to the applause of bystanders.

The captain, seeing what happened, rushed down to make sure the man was all right, "That was a tremendous leap," the captain said, "but if you waited for just another minute, we would have docked, and you could have walked on."

Imagine! This Herculean effort to be on time and our commuter didn't even notice if the ferry was coming or going. Let's face it. There are days we tear around in a blind rush not at all sure if we're coming or going. Admit it. Just commuting back and forth to work is part of the daily grind that keeps the rat race alive in your life.

> Let's face it! There are days we tear about in a blind rush...

THE RUSH FACTOR

Let's imagine for the moment that you and I are attending a college class aimed at explaining America's rush-factor. Our professor announces today's lecture is, "A Modern Perspective on Punctuality." It sounds simple enough and the professor gets her class underway with the following problem:

> Mr. Smith must attend an important business meeting 30 miles from home. His sales presentation will open the meeting for a prospective client so being on time is crucial. The meeting is scheduled for Monday morning at 10:00 A.M.

The professor indicates Mr. Smith's rush-factor is directly proportional to his driving speed in order to arrive at his meeting on time. What's immediately evident is that his rush-factor will fluctuate depending on how much travel time he allows himself.

With a flourish of blue marker the professor writes across the whiteboard:

> Mr. Smith's rush-factor equals minutes remaining until his appointment, divided by velocity required to arrive on time.

With a bold red marker she scrawls the relevant equation:

$$Rf = T/V$$

Dutifully, we jot down the equation in our notebooks. Concluding her lecture she divides the class into pairs. The assignment is to develop an alternate approach for illustrating life's rush-factor. You and I decide to convert her equation into a graph supported by an accompanying table of figures. A few head scratches later, we complete our task. Our chart turns out to be:

Distance to Meeting	Time Leaving for Meeting	Available Travel Time in Minutes	Ratio of Speed to Punctuality (mile/min)	Speed Required to Arrive on Time
30 miles	9:00	60	0.5	30 mph
	9:10	50	0.6	36 mph
	9:20	40	0.75	45 mph
	9:30	30	1	60 mph
	9:40	20	1.5	90 mph
	9:50	10	3	180 mph

Our supporting graph works out as:

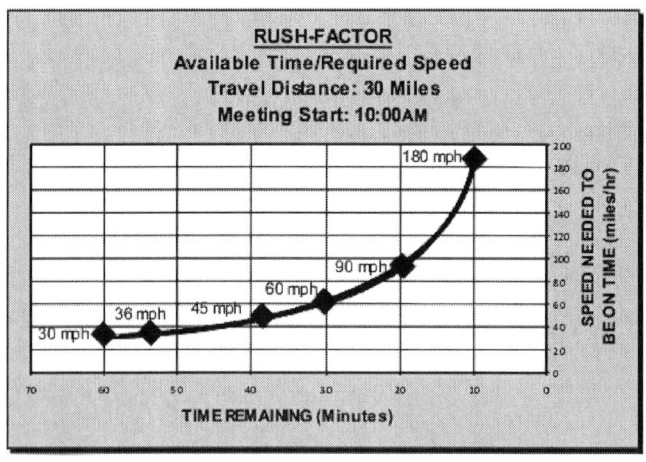

As our charts show, a person's rush-factor dramatically increases as available travel time decreases. To put it another way, Mr. Smith's rush-factor is inversely proportional to the time remaining before the start of his meeting. In other words: less time greater hurry. With 60 minutes remaining before his appointment, Mr. Smith can drive a leisurely 30mph. Cut that time in half and he'll need to double his speed to arrive on time. As a result, his rush-factor has doubled. By pushing the envelope and leaving only twenty minutes travel time Mr. Smith is forced to drive a ticket-gathering 90mph to arrive on time. His rush-factor has now tripled. In other words, he's racing.

Granted, we already know all this so let's go ahead and score ourselves an A+ for the class. How well aware we are that the more we try to squeeze into a fixed amount of time the faster we must fly to get everything done—and most times without ever noticing if life's ferry is coming or going.

Take the morning routine. For many families it's a gauntlet they run to get out of the house on time. The all-to-familiar shouts of "hurry up" at the bathroom door, or "I don't have time now," while bolting out the front door are hallmarks of the morning rush. With barely enough time to make it to work or drop the kids off at school, you jump in the car, fasten your seatbelt, and start down the road only to discover the gas gauge is on empty. Suddenly your rush-factor jumps ten-points (to say nothing of your blood pressure). A stop for a fill up now means you're running late. Listen! A horn blast in the distance. Life's ferry is nearing the dock. The urge to run

> Suddenly your rush-factor jumps ten points...

surges. Your worst fear mounts—you may miss the boat!

THE STRESS FACTOR

Doctors now warn of a direct link between the accelerated pace of contemporary living and higher stress levels that adversely affect our health. At today's pace of trying to fit 32 hours of living into a 24-hour day is it any wonder that "stressed out" has become a common colloquialism? Like our New York commuter, we frantically spin our wheels with near disastrous results.

One airport baggage handler had an interesting way to relieve his occupational stress. Besieged by an irate traveler the curbside porter remained calm and cheerful despite the verbal abuse for how he handled the man's luggage. The infuriated traveler finally stormed off. A woman who witnessed the encounter approached the porter.

> ...we are frantically spinning our wheels with near disastrous results

"I'm curious," she said. "How did you manage to stay so calm with that man?"

"It's easy," replied baggage handler. "That guy's going to New York—I'm sending his bags to Brazil."

Ahh...if it was only that easy for the rest of us to eliminate our stress.

A few years back, United Parcel Service had a slogan that well defined our times. They affirmed

UPS was "moving at the speed of business." Today the "speed of business" is approaching warp drive. We live in a world of drive-through windows, instant rebates, same-day deliveries, microwaved meals, and instant banking by smartphone.

Several years ago, one TV advertiser embraced the accelerated flow of life as a positive thing. With a background of syncopated music and motion, representing a well orchestrated accelerated life, one shopper attempts using cash instead of a Visa card. The music suddenly stops and shoppers freeze in place. The message is loud and clear: faster is better and Visa is faster than money.

It was inevitable that America would progress from Pony Express to Federal Express; from frontier railway to airport runway. It's obvious; our culture now runs in a vortex of hurry. Those idyllic "Andy of Mayberry" days of a slower lifestyle have effectively vanished along with our black and white television sets. Unable to regain an elusive past, our efforts are now focused on keeping our hurried world from draining us physically, emotionally, and spiritually.

> Our culture obviously runs in a vortex of hurry.

Stephen Convey makes an interesting point on the cultural expectations of our day in his book, *First Things First*. He observes,

> People expect us to be busy, overworked. It's become a status symbol in our society—if we're busy, we're important; if we're not busy,

we're embarrassed to admit it. Busyness is where we get our security, It's validating, popular and pleasing, It's also a good excuse for not dealing with the first things in our lives.[1]

We are driven to be busy by a cultural standard that drains every ounce of our vitality, along with our hope of ever finding peace and contentment. Then somewhere in the midst of our rushed lives, physically and emotionally exhausted, we stop to catch our breath and question the value of keeping up with a world demanding that we buy more, try more, and fly more.

Listen! A horn blast in the distance. Life's ferry is nearing the dock. The urge to run surges. Your worst fear mounts—you may miss the boat!

YOUNG AND OLD ALIKE

For those like myself entering life's winter season there's a strong compulsion to hurry for an entirely different reason than "keeping up with the Joneses." This sense of urgency stems from the awareness that time is quickly slipping away. Those of us reaching into our fifties, sixties, or beyond feel pressured to realize lifelong ambitions before it's...well...too late. We find ourselves double-checking our proverbial bucket list. Efforts to accomplish long-held goals

> Unlike the long summers of our youth, time is now a precious commodity.

keep nipping at our heels like a tenacious Chihuahua. Unlike the long summers of our youth, time is now a precious commodity.

The years that make up our lives steadily move in one direction. Much like our New York commuter who learned the ferry runs on a tight schedule, the ship of our life's labors also sails on a strict timetable; only in our case there are no stops until that final port of call.

Life does not come with a pause button on a remote control. The sand within the hourglass of our days is constantly running down. The next page on life's calendar must be turned. Making matters worse, time slips by faster as we grow older. And this sense of accelerated time attacks with even greater intensity the older we get. We're driven to finish what must be done.

On the other end of life's spectrum, youth is often driven to move faster by the outside forces of company demands. A thinning workforce along with the priority for increased profits all contribute to the fevered pace of corporate America. There's an inescapable (typically non-verbal) pressure driving employees to work faster and harder to meet increasing company demands. Many personnel now carry the workload once shared by laid-off employees. Fearful of a layoff themselves many are working in overdrive with a self-sacrificing commitment to overtime and corporate expectations. Add raising children and running a household to the mix and you've hit the top end of life's speedometer.

Besides the outside influence of corporate life, an inner drive for success propels workers full speed down life's highway. Is it any wonder that in the midst of relentless pressure to succeed many feel a greater need for emotional relief than physical rest? Caught up in the cultural flow, there's a real need to anchor ourselves to something secure and unyielding. Many are longing for some assurance that the raging currents of life will not sweep them downstream into the ever circling eddies of hopeless despair. Such assurance comes from a solid hope that stands up to the compelling pressure to submit our sensibilities to the fevered pace. 📖

Seeing Things as They Really Are

> "If everybody minded their own business the world would go round a deal faster than it does."
> —The Duchess
> *Alice's Adventures in Wonderland*, Lewis Carroll

When our granddaughter first began to talk, one of her favorite words at dinner was, "more!" It's a typical sentiment, not only from young children, but from many adults as well. We live in a culture of more. We have been led to believe the abundant life is found in acquiring more. More of what you ask? More of everything…more house, more car, more clothes, larger TVs, upgraded cell phones, more tools, more toys…ad infinitum. We are rushing headlong over the precipice to get, as someone aptly put it, "more stuff." One anonymous poet addressed this modern malady with this bit of humor:

> We get and buy, and buy and get;
> It fills our homes and storage, yet
> It never seems to be enough;
> We're still collecting other stuff.

Despite its allure, possessing all the right stuff

has never been the pathway to contentment, fulfillment, or meaningful living. The fallacy of such thinking is obvious once we own those things we so strongly desired. We quickly discover that tomorrow reveals new desires to be satisfied; new longings to be fulfilled, and new products to buy.

If it's HD TV this year, then it's 3D TV next year. If it's an iPhone 7 this year, then it's an iPhone 8 next year. For this reason alone the pace of life will never slow down. We're too busy buying the next best thing.

If our hope for finding contentment lies solely in getting more stuff then, without question, this world of incessant hurry to keep up will fail to deliver. Knowing the human heart is never satisfied, is it any wonder that Jesus addressed this very issue when he warned, "Beware…for not even when one has an abundance does his life consist of his possessions" (Luke 12:15 NASB).

Materialism cannot help but fall short of providing the abundant life—a life of peace and contentment—for the simple reason it cannot satisfy our deepest need for acceptance, love, and purpose. Such things cannot be bought at Walmart, Macy's, or on Rodeo Drive in Beverly Hills. Purchases of any sort are a poor substitute for companionship, nurturing self-worth, or appreciation for life's simple pleasures.

In our rush for more, life gives way to the anxiety that accompanies the accumulation of wealth and possessions. Subtly, our possessions begin to possess us. We become enslaved to their maintenance, repairs, upgrades, and monthly payments. Best-selling author Randy Alcorn, founder and director of Eternal Perspectives Ministries, makes this observation:

> Materialism is the mother of anxiety. No wonder Christ's discourse on earthly and heavenly treasures is immediately followed by his admonitions not to worry about material things (Matthew 6:25-34). People lay up treasures on earth rather than in heaven not only because of greed and selfishness, but also because of fear and insecurity. Yet putting our hope in earthly treasures does nothing but multiply anxiety. Why? Because our earthly treasures are so temporary and uncertain.
>
> The hopes of a person with primary investments in the stock market will rise and fall with the market. The one whose greatest riches are deposited in the bank will be destroyed when the banks fail, as will the farmer whose greatest asset is in crops when the crops fail or when the commodity markets fall. In contrast, the one whose hope is in God will be devastated only if God fails—and he never does.[2]

As long as materialism stubbornly remains the focus of our lives spirituality remains in the shadows. The accumulation of things falls far short in providing the eternal value of personal significance or a worthwhile purpose for our existence.

Charles Swindoll takes note of Alexander Whyte's observation of our tendency to *"hang very heavy weights on very thin wires."* He writes:

> We hang the very heavy weights of our peace on the very thin wire of our possessions. We know better, but we still do it. Materialistic to the core, we convince ourselves that life *does* consist in the abundance of things we possess...that contentment is *not* limited to food and clothing...that the birds of the air and the lilies of the field don't know what they're missing without all those creature comforts.[3]

Materialism is seductive in its appeal, but fails on its promise to provide peace and contentment for two essential reasons. First, the human heart is never satisfied. It constantly craves for more. What satisfies today leaves us discontented tomorrow. Consequently, an endless pursuit for bigger, or better, or newer, is always at work within us. Secondly, and more importantly, true contentment finds its essence, not in the material side of life, but in the spiritual side of life.

Benjamin Franklin understood the futility of clinging to a hope solely fixed within our hurried world when he penned: "He that lives upon hope dies fasting."

Some years ago an acquaintance of mine earned a generous six-figure salary as a chemical analyst. As the result of corporate downsizing he was laid off from his high paying position. For several long years he diligently looked for work in his field. Finally, out of economic desperation, he took a job at Home Depot. There was no getting around the fact his financial situation had drastically changed.

Knowing him as I did his hope for happiness and his purpose in life were not tightly wrapped up in his career. If that had been the case, he likely would have suffered a resounding personal defeat that may have spiraled into clinical depression. Instead, his hope was fixed upon spiritual principles. He believed life held a higher purpose than to merely satisfy personal ambitions. And yes, he traveled the rough road of disappointment. At times his emotions were drained until only a keen discouragement remained—but he was never defeated. He embraced and maintained a spiritual perspective on life. His trust in God never wavered.

Nothing in this hurried world is guaranteed. Just ask those who once worked for or invested in World-Com, Global Crossing, or Enron. Ask those affected by the bankruptcy of the multi-billion dollar investment bank of Lehman Brothers in 2009. With a debt of $613 billion their Chapter 13 bankruptcy filing marked the largest in U.S. history. During this same year the stock market had the worst week in its 112-year history. The Dow Jones Industrials tumbled from its record high of nearly 14,000 in 2007 to half that volume two years later. It was the darkest days on both Wall Street and Main Street since the Great Depression.

The United States was not alone in its troubles;

market indicators fell around the globe. Financial leaders from the world's industrialized nations met in an effort to reverse the trend and find workable solutions to jump-start the world economy. Without question, a hope that relies solely upon financial markets is worrisome at best.

MADISON AVENUE PSYCHOLOGY

Like a magnet, we are irresistibly drawn to the material side of life as our vehicle of hope for finding life's best. The current trend of advertising reflects this high value we place on tangible commodities. Years ago, advertisers were content to simply extol the virtues of their products that provided cleaner clothes, fresher food, or an opportunity to "see the USA in your Chevrolet." No longer. The last five decades have seen a dynamic shift in the philosophy of many advertisers. Subtly they ask us to believe the inherent value of their products goes far beyond their evident use; that their products can satisfy the core needs of the human heart. These advertisers are no longer selling goods; they are merchandising hope. Sadly, their efforts to convince us that happiness and self worth are just a purchase away utterly ignores the spiritual reality that is part of our existence.

Some years ago one company promoted their

product as a means of restoring basic family values. They were selling a quick-fix hope that their quick-fix meals would restore the traditional family dinner around the dining room table.

Another example of merchandising hope and happiness came from the now defunct General Motors Pontiac line that for years, told us they "build excitement" (like we need more of that). At one point their advertising slogan proclaimed Pontiac was "fuel for the soul."

Make no mistake; the philosophy of the advertising industry is well beyond merely selling products. They dive deep into the human psyche baiting the consumer with a hope of satisfying more than those basic needs for food, clothing, and shelter.

> ...the philosophy of advertising industry is well beyond merely selling products.

One company worked hard to persuade its customers that exceptional self-image is wrapped up in their clothing line. Another advertiser went so far as to tell us, "Image is everything." One cosmetic company endeavors to bolster every woman's ego by saying, "You're worth it." Marketing gurus now see themselves as promoting, not simply tangible merchandise for the consumer, but the intangible commodities of happiness, contentment, personal fulfillment, and self-worth. In short, hope for a perfect and happy life is just a purchase away.

Yet theirs is an empty promise. We've used their detergents, driven their cars, and worn their name-brand clothes. And when you get right down to it, we're no happier now (or sexier; or more accepted by our peers) than before. To be sure, our purchases have delivered on life's little pleasures and physical necessities, but all along our hope was for those purchases—especially those big-ticket items of houses and cars—would prove to be that missing piece of the puzzle we crave deep in our souls.

THE MATERIAL VS. THE SPIRITUAL

A critical need exists in our culture to acknowledge the spiritual side of life. While any purchase holds *intrinsic* value, it inherently lacks *spiritual* value. What the heart craves most cannot be found in a purchase. The key to meaningful living and peace of mind is found beyond the next purchase. Materialism offers little more than a temporary slice of pleasure hoping to satisfy our deepest longings. No matter how well meaning, hoping to find serenity in a purchase is a fleeting feeling at best.

The new car, the new carpet, or the remodeled kitchen cannot erase the gnawing emptiness of life in the fast lane. That initial excitement from the novelty of a new possession eventually fades. What's left is typically little more than the monthly payments. Subsequently, it's only a matter of time before our longing-for-something-else resurfaces.

Discontentment is inevitable when our efforts to find substantive living are woven tightly to material things. Our hearts yearn for a hope in something that goes beyond the façade of the empty promises of consumerism. We thirst for something that truly satisfies the soul.

> Whether he articulates it or not, the natural man the world over is crying, "I thirst." Why this consuming desire to acquire wealth? Why this craving for the honors...? Why the mad rush after pleasure, the turn from one form of it to another with persistent and unwearied diligence? Why this eager search for wisdom—this scientific inquiry, this pursuit of philosophy...and this ceaseless experimentation by the moderns? Why the insane craze for that which is novel? Why? Because there is an aching void in the soul. Because there is something remaining in every natural man that is *unsatisfied*. This is true of the millionaire equally as much as the pauper: the riches of the former bring no real contentment. It is as true of the globetrotter equally as much as of the country rustic who has never been outside the bounds of his native country: traveling from one end of the earth to the other and back again, he fails to discover the secret of peace.[4]

This "secret of peace" is found nowhere else but in a personal relationship with our Creator. This relationship is the key to genuine and eternal significance. It provides us with a sense of acceptance and belonging, as well as peace of mind. Here is where the soul finds rest and satisfaction. Settled upon God's faultless character and unfailing promises, hope springs alive. Ultimately, that new car or remodeled kitchen is a poor substitute for a personal relationship with the living God.

In his book, *What Ever Happened to the American Dream*, Larry Burkett blames the lost American dream to a lost hope that was once tied to God. He notes:

> We, as a people, are facing some enormous challenges and problems of our own making. In reality, the short-term economic problems we face are not more severe than those faced by previous generations of Americans…The difference between those generations and ours is a basic attitude called "hope." The people of past eras had confidence (hope) that things would get better and faith that God was still with them. On the other hand, we live in a generation that has been subjected to so much media brainwashing that government, not God, is our resource. And hope is waning.[5]

The irony of our technological age is that we have more of everything temporal but less of anything substantial. For the most part, our needs and many wants are met, but there remains a growing barrenness of soul; our possessions ring hollow. A sense of futility overshadows our endeavors. Regrettably, some run that much faster hoping to escape such feelings by volunteering for yet another project, joining another organization, changing careers, or turning shop-a-holic, all in the hope of gratifying their deepest need for finding true satisfaction.

In the midst of our passion to live life to its fullest something has now awakened. Perhaps for the first time, we are aware that keeping pace with this hurried world is not the solution. We are finally seeing things as they really are. It's the spiritual side of life that's all-important in our quest for finding that missing piece of life's puzzle: a hope rooted in the divine.

When God's promises become the object of our hope then emotional calm and spiritual strength replace stress and turmoil. We find tranquility in the midst of life's whirlwind. We are relieved of that overwhelming feeling of being swept away, beyond the edge of sanity, by the rush of frantic living. This anonymous paraphrase of Psalm 23 offers a fresh perspective on living in the presence of God:

> The Lord is my pacesetter, I shall not rush. He makes me stop and rest at intervals. He provides me with images of stillness to restore my serenity. He leads me in the way of efficiency to calmness of mind and His guidance is peace. Even though I have a great many things to accomplish this day, I will not fret for His presence is here. His timeliness,

His all importance will keep me in balance. He prepares refreshment and renewal in the midst of my activity, anointing my head with the oils of tranquility. My cup of joyous energy overflows. Surely harmony and effectiveness shall be the fruits of my hours, for I shall walk in the pace of my Lord and dwell in His heaven forever.

In his classic book, *Knowing God*, J.I. Packer confronts our sensibilities:

> We are cruel to ourselves if we try to live in this world without knowing about the God whose world it is and who runs it. The world becomes a strange, mad, painful place, and life in it a disappointing and unpleasant business, for those who do not know about God. Disregard the study of God, and you sentence yourself to stumble and blunder through life blindfolded, as it were, with no sense of direction and no understanding of what surrounds you. [6]

When Monkeys Run Wild

"To Carthage I came, where there sang all around me in my ears a cauldron of unholy loves."
—*The Confessions*; Augustine

Hope must have an object to keep its spark of life alive. It cannot exist alone. In his book, *Living on the Ragged Edge*, Charles Swindoll observes:

> Why do they keep telling us to look for light at the end of the tunnel? Why do people conduct great seminars all around the world and tell people to smile more, to believe 'there's a bright, beautiful tomorrow...just grab for it...go for the gusto...hitch your wagon to a star...you'll make it someday'? You know why they tell us those things? There's one simple answer: to make us believe there's purpose and happiness if we simply keep on hoping. But hope cannot exist in a vacuum where facts are ignored. 7

Realizing hope must be tied to something—*anything*—our tendency is to tie it to the tangible rather than the spiritual. We gravitate toward that which we can see and feel. The trouble is, nothing in this world is permanent. By its very nature, that which is tangible forms a weak foundation for abiding hope. Consider where people typically place their hope:

- Health
- Money
- Family
- Careers
- Position or Power
- Natural abilities
- Human reasoning
- Government

At best this list presents a tenuous basis for a real and enduring hope. A hope solely dependent upon man's ability to eliminate hardship, improve circumstances, or cure a disease may suffice for those advances possible through our learned abilities; but reality shows that humanity is neither all-powerful nor all-knowing. The question then becomes: will the hope we hold sustain us when, in spite of all our efforts, solutions are not found? A hope wholly reliant upon the frailties of the human condition to consistently provide a life lived "happily ever after" is fertile ground for discouragement, skepticism, heartbreak, or worse.

With hope no higher than our humanity, how do we answer the young wife asking why she's left alone with three small children following her husband's untimely death. What consolation do we offer those now facing a terminal illness? How do we comfort the son or daughter whose parent has been stolen by Alzheimer's disease? How do we console the wife who, after twenty-five years of marriage, finds her husband has just walked out on her? How do we respond to the parent whose child has been diagnosed with leukemia or cerebral palsy? Without our hope abiding in an all-powerful, all-knowing, and all-loving God we are at a loss for answers to life's harshest realities.

FACING THE FACTS

Our lives can be instantly transformed. All it takes is a doctor's diagnosis of cancer; a midnight call from police; or an unexpected layoff. Lou Gehrig is a classic example of a man whose life was abruptly turned upside down. This longstanding baseball hero was unexpectedly struck down at the height of a successful sports career with ALS, a disease now bearing his name.

Hollywood celebrity, Michael J. Fox, is another example of someone's health being stolen by a malevolent illness. At the height of his film career, while only in his mid-thirties, he developed Parkinson's disease. Despite the long-term prognosis he remains optimistic that science will eventually find a cure. Within ten years he sees more effective drugs becoming available that will minimize the effects of the disease. He spearheaded the Michael J. Fox Foundation for Parkinson's Research, which has already raised over $150 million in efforts to cure the disease. He has accurately defined hope by saying, "Hope is optimism tied to facts."[8] Fox hits the nail on the head. Any hope of substance must

> A meaningful hope must be anchored to something solid.

be tied to facts rather than wishful thinking.

Science has made great strides in eliminating scores of deadly diseases. Ailments that have plagued humanity for centuries have been eradicated, and the work continues. Currently a vaccine for malaria, which annually kills tens of thousands, is under human testing and is slated to be put into worldwide use within five years. Without question, human misery has been dramatically reduced through scientific breakthroughs.

> A solid mooring *is* available in this ever-changing world.

Good as this news is, some diseases remain incurable, most notably those from genetic defects. Moreover, lives continue to be torn apart by personal tragedy, divorce, unemployment, wayward children, or crushing debt. Problems persistantly plague us. There's always the fighting chance things will improve. But at some point we realize not every problem will find its solution, not every tragedy will end in triumph, and not every heart will change for the better. And neither will the rat-race ever slow down.

Yet something positive remains. A solid mooring *is* available in this ever-changing world. It is no further away than the best selling book of all time—the Bible. A hope settled upon those spiritual realities laid out in the Bible has an unwavering stability, for it stands upon an eternally firm foundation.

THE SERPENT OF SEDUCTION

Seductive forces are constantly at work luring us away from a hope in God and His Word. One such temptress is the goddess of consumerism. Her enticements are bright and shimmering trappings. But when the spotlight of spiritual reality is turned on, we see her for what she really is—empty packaging. Heartfelt peace, real security, and legitimate self-worth are missing from beneath her colorful trappings.

She is not alone however, a second temptress confronts us as well. Her allure is far more cunning than the overt trappings of consumerism. Her trimmings are not as flamboyant as her attractive sibling, but they are nevertheless just as persuasive. Rather than appealing to the eye, this subtle seductress appeals to the mind. Like the Sirens of Greek mythology her song is irresistible.

Multitudes are spellbound by her melodic appeal that hope for a better and fuller life lies solely in science and education. Yet she fails to answer those four questions that have haunted humanity for millennia: Where did we come from? Does life have meaning? What happens after death? Is there a God?

In the first of my two college careers I came face-to-face with the teachings of evolution through a Physical Anthropology class. Captivated I listened as the Sirens of academia sang. Research papers were eventually assigned. I determined to immerse myself with unrelenting passion into the probing question of the origin of life. My resulting thesis was entitled, *The Chemical Theory of Abiogenesis*. The study heralded the supposed fact that life originated from non-living molecules comprised of amino acids. I relished this opportunity to explore one of the fundamental "truths" of the universe. At the time I was an avid believer in the molecule-to-monkey-to-man theory, or as someone quipped, "the blob to Bob" theory. But for all its short-lived glory, my research project conveyed nothing more than a philosophy of hopeless despair. Lingering questions remained. Despite all its scientific jargon and comprehensive suppositions, it made but a single point: what you see is all the reality that exists; we are here by random chance and nothing more. The opening line from Carl Sagan's bestseller, *Cosmos*, accurately summed up my belief at the time, "The cosmos is all that is or ever was or ever will be."

In the end, my thesis amounted to a philosophical "so what?" I had found no satisfactory answers to life's deepest questions; neither had my efforts offered a hope of any kind. Ultimately, evolution teaches humanity is nothing more than a series of genetic mutations ever climbing toward a higher order of species.

> My thesis simply amounted to a philosophical "so what?"

In retrospect the zookeeper of evolutionary thinking was feeding the newly emerging decadence of the 1960s. Morality and spirituality had been shanghaied by academia and locked within a cage of silence. At the same time the monkeys of cultural mayhem borne of theoretical science were now running wild on college campuses, and soon spilled into the nation's streets.

The quality of life once founded upon moral traditions stemming from a biblical foundation has all but been replaced with a hedonistic philosophy resulting in a cultural decline to this present hour. For years our society has been steadily sinking into the morass of sensuality accompanied by a growing sense of despair regarding our future. The law of the jungle is now being played out on the streets of our nation. Even our standards of entertainment have fallen to an all-time low portraying graphic violence and overt sexuality. The Sirens of science and academia are still singing and America is still listening.

In the midst of those early college days one nagging question stood out in my mind—does God exist? Following my graduation came marriage, work, and life in general, all of which pushed that prime question out of mind.

Years later a co-worker casually swept an arm across the panoramic view of a summer's day and unexpectedly asked me, "How do you suppose all this got here?" I thought the question odd at the time, but armed with the "evidence" I was ready for a discussion on the subject of origins. I voiced my belief and followed up with a detailed explanation of how, in the course of billions of years, the dust and gases from the big bang and its formation of the universe condensed into stars and planets: so I had been taught and so I preached. His reply to what I proudly considered a thorough and accurate answer came as a shock. This hardened construction worker simply said, "I believe God made it all." I was caught off guard. This was the first time I ever heard someone bring God so casually into a conversation. A straightforward conviction resonated in his voice. It amazed me. He firmly believed what he said. And just that quickly he started me thinking about that long-forgotten question of mine.

Following that discussion a series of related events brought me to the place where I also embraced a belief in the God of creation. I accepted the biblical account of origins. But something else took place at that time. At long last, my college-age question was answered. I finally understood that life's real meaning lies beyond the physical realm. A living hope was born within me. 📖

Part 2
Gaining Direction

Fear often drowns hope. Basically, there are two types of fear in this world: the fear of dying and the fear of circumstances. Modern wisdom says, conquer these fears and hope will return. God's wisdom says, Have hope and these fears will die. Hope is not the result of gaining victory over our fears, but is instead the means of gaining the victory.

—Anonymous

Discovering Living Hope

> Have all the hopes of ages come to naught?
> Is life no more with noble meaning fraught?
> — Ada Cambridge

A sunrise silhouette of Providence, Rhode Island greets me as I look out from the top floor of the hospital. I'm anxiously waiting for the doctor's report following my wife's surgery. A myriad of thoughts are racing through my mind in the early morning hours. Mainly I'm focused on how quickly life can change.

I retreat from the window and survey the room. The placard on the wall identifies the lounge area as *The Healing Garden*. Comfortably furnished with several overstuffed chairs, half a dozen deep-seated couches, and a few tables, it's an area where people can congregate or individuals can find therapeutic solitude. A computer and a large aquarium occupy one corner of the room. Parked along the opposite wall is an upright piano. On it sits a solitary book.

Curious, I retrieve the volume. I'm surprised to find I'm holding a public journal. Evidently it's available for those who want to inscribe their thoughts or prayers onto its blank pages. Leafing through the journal I discover dozens of heartfelt inscriptions. The majority of its anonymous entries are brief but poignant. Many are petitions of prayer for family members undergoing surgery. Other entries express gratitude to God for successful operations, while a few held expressions of thanksgiving for healthy births. One young man wrote:

Dear God,
Thank you for a beautiful, healthy Italian baby girl.

I couldn't help but smile. Surely this father would have been just as thankful if God had somehow given him a healthy *Irish* baby girl.

I continue leafing through the pages. Amid dozens of inscriptions, either thanking God or seeking His help, I discover one deeply solemn entry. This anonymous family had evidently been battered by one of life's fiercest storms. Yet, on the horizon of life's turbulent seas an encouraging thought surfaces. Perhaps circumstances would eventually steer them into calmer waters. But as life would have it, that single prayer they felt made it through to God only resulted in "more wind and waves." They pen no details. The entry reminds me of the dichotomy that exists within every hospital; on the one hand its ability to heal the sick, on the other hand, its inability save every life. This family's expectation of renewed health for their loved one was seemingly thrust upon rocky shores. Their emotions were in turmoil. Any hope for a recovery was evidently pinned to nothing more than a wavering optimism. Their entry reads:

> Our ship has been lost at sea for some time. The wind and the waves have crashed and pushed their way into our lives. Our tattered sails have deflected prayer after prayer from being delivered. At the moment of all lost hope, one time a heartfelt prayer made its way to our Maker.
>
> In turn the answer was more wind and waves. Unknowing the answered prayer, fear gripped our hearts as the boat narrowly missed rocks and reefs. In respect to the sea we were nothing. A family lost in fear and unnoticed by the storm around us. At a distance maybe faith, maybe false hope—light shines down in bright unbroken beams. You feel the wind, you feel the waves. You feel your heart full of anxious longing not felt since a child. Maybe we are moving in the right direction.

Their words crush down on the soul. You sense the enormous weight upon the heart of this family. They hold no real assurance. Their only hope is that "maybe" circumstances were improving; "maybe" they were "moving in the right direction."

Many of us can identify with this hurting family. At times we find our own hope slipping away. Yet from deep within our soul there wells up an optimism that claims, "maybe" circumstances *will* change, or prayers *will* be answered, or personal battles *will* be won. We remain, in a word, hopeful.

Within all of us there resides an optimism that the future will be better—brighter—blessed. We are confident that failure can turn into success, broken lives can be mended, and hopeless situations can be turned around.

Thomas Carlyle (1795-1881), the Scottish essayist once wrote, "Man is, properly speaking, based upon hope; he has no other possession but hope; this world of his is emphatically the place of hope."

In the midst of our trials and tribulations each sunrise offers the hope of a new beginning; a fresh start; a second chance. The recurrence of the seasons has taught us that hidden within the barren winter lives the hope of a returning spring. Each birth kindles a hope for a better world. Every true friend offers the hope of encouragement and help in time of need. Each medical breakthrough offers the hope of alleviating human suffering or curing another debilitating disease.

Such optimism is rooted in the fact that mankind once resided in Paradise. From the beginning we were meant to live in a world of unhurried tranquility and contentment—where things *always* turned out right and suffering and evil were unknown. Evidently something has gone horribly wrong. The proof is all around us; distress, despair, and death envelop our world like a dark shroud. With each passing year we spin our wheels faster only to sink deeper into loneliness, bitterness, or hopelessness. Clearly we have fallen from Eden.

Nevertheless a trace of Paradise remains, well proven by why we shun the pain and turmoil that invades our lives. Intuitively we sense there is something better, not only for the world at large but for ourselves as well. We remain hopeful that what was once lost will somehow be restored. Our anxious longing for all things to turn out right leads us down the path of eternal optimism. This is the hope that makes us tick.

Our deepest desire is for our lives to read, "And they lived happily ever after." Experience teaches us however that life can turn out any way but happy. Yet even in our darkest hour the call of Eden resonates in our soul. We refuse to resign ourselves to a fatalistic view. Our tendency is to firmly believe that better times are on the way; and if not soon, then certainly someday. This God-given optimism is ingrained in every human heart. It's a quality shared the world over.

> Our deepest desire is for our lives to read, "They lived happily ever after."

While the human race is consummately

hopeful, when faced with a prolonged or overwhelming hardship the brightest optimism can fade. Hope's sunlight easily slips behind the storm clouds of tragedy. Distress has a way of enrobing us in emotional darkness. We begin drifting upon the shadowy waters of a moonless sea. We are troubled by the thought that circumstances may not turn out in our favor. Instead of a hope offering security and confidence we unwittingly end up clinging to a "maybe" just as our unnamed family above. Uncertainty boldly takes center stage in our lives, making us insecure about the future.

We all desire to be the masters of our own fate. We want the power to effectually change unpleasant circumstances, gratify our desires, and fulfill our own aspirations. This desire for mastery is nothing new. Back in the Garden of Eden Eve faced this same temptation to take control by taking the forbidden fruit when Satan told her she could be like God. In disobeying God and seizing that one controlling moment she paid a far higher price than she ever imagined.

> We all desire to be the masters of our own fate.

If the foundation of our hope remains only in our ability to maintain control over the events in our lives then, like Eve, we are destined for the greatest of disappointments. None of us are able to eliminate every hardship or unpleasant eventuality that crosses our path. Genuine hope does not rest upon having power to manipulate circumstances or people. Hope's heartbeat originates with God; its every breath comes by accepting His unfailing promises.

I continue reading through the hospital journal. A few pages later, I find a vibrant illustration of living hope. Clearly this next writer possessed an unwavering conviction that life holds significant meaning, real purpose, and a glorious future. No "maybe" intrudes into this entry. Only a confident optimism revealing a heartfelt assurance that despite any solution being out of their hands, God remains in control.

> No "maybe" intrudes into this entry.

For this individual, hope was not dependent upon seeing difficulties change, but instead focused upon an unchanging God. This writer boldly affirms their faith in Jesus Christ. Their unwavering belief was that Jesus is the single source of meaningful hope. They write:

> To my dear and precious Jesus,
> It's good to know we have you in these difficult times we go through; that you're there beside us, comforting us and strengthening those weak areas...You are the one we have hope in and you are the one to look to for victory...

What a stark contrast to the earlier entry with its smattering of wishful thinking that "maybe" the storms would subside; "maybe" things would work out; "maybe" the surgery would be successful.

DETOURS HAPPEN

The smooth road of our own desires may be blocked one day forcing us onto one of life's detours. When that happens our need is for a hope that will suffice when the highway of our dreams and aspirations is regrettably fading from sight in the rear view mirror. We want a hope that will support us when and life's detour leads us away from our desired direction.

In 1988 my father was forced onto one of life's detours. As a mechanical engineer from the World War II generation, he recognized the importance of keeping pace with an ever-changing world. Coming from the age of drafting boards and T-squares, the advent of personal computers forced my father to recognize his mode of work was hopelessly outdated. In his affable way he determined to keep up with the changing times. At the age of sixty-two he enrolled in a local college resolved to learn Computer-Aided Drafting (CAD). What is now an industry standard was at that time a revolution to designers, engineers, and architects.

> The smooth road of our own desires may be blocked one day…

My father invested a remarkable amount of work in his effort to succeed. The first obstacle he needed to overcome was to learn to operate a computer. Only then could he jump into the challenge of learning his job as an engineer with software rather than a T-square. He was determined to prove an "old dog" could learn new tricks. He steadily progressed and in time graduated from the program. Shortly afterwards, he was hired by a small company not far from our rural home in the farmlands of northern New Jersey. Life was proceeding as planned. Like a small boy with a new toy he relished plying his trade by means of high technology. His new job was barely started when the unexpected detour came through a diagnosis of lung cancer. For a man who never smoked it was a bitter pill to swallow.

Like thousands of others on the same detour of cancer each year, he eagerly sought for a cure. Though aggressive steps of treatment were taken, a cure never came. Long months stretched into a couple of hard years. Eventually it became evident my father was living out his last days. His hope no longer rested in a miraculous recovery. Instead it rested upon God. In the end, my father's hope was settled upon God's promise of eternal life through Jesus Christ. His hope and mine rested in the reality that he and I would once again meet on a brighter and happier shore.

Life has the bad habit of bypassing our road of expectations. Detours callously compel us onto unexpected side roads. Powerless to turn back we are forced to travel into an unforeseen future.

Anxiety becomes an uninvited passenger. In poetic fashion Washington Gladden describes a detour taken in his own life:

> In the bitter waves of woe,
> Beaten and tossed about;
> By the sullen winds that blow
> From the desolate shore of doubt.
> Where the anchors that faith has cast
> Are dragging in the gale,
> I am quietly holding fast
> To the things that cannot fail.

The detours of life are real. Poor health, lost jobs, financial hardships, broken families, or broken dreams are all detours that force us to reexamine our basis of hope. Growing numbers are on the detour of caring for aging parents or a chronically ill spouse or child. They have long ago given up their expectations of either a medical or miraculous cure. What they possess instead is a hope that cannot be crushed under the weight of insurmountable tragedy. Fighting life's grim battle only strengthens their belief in God, and that one day He will right all the wrongs of this world.

Their eyes are fixed upon Him. He is the source of their strength for the difficult journey. He encourages the heart and soothes the mind and is the author of a living hope that remains unyielding though lives may be buffeted by the winds of misfortune. Here then is a hope that can satisfy our greatest desires, alleviate our deepest fears, and carry us over the roughest of roads while shining the light of truth on our darkest detours.

This rushed and broken world is incapable of supplying a hope that will stand up to those painful detours that lead us into an unknown future. A "maybe" simply will not do if we long for absolute peace of mind and a genuine contentment of soul. The solution is to grab hold of that which is firm and steadfast. Sensing our troubled heart and restless soul Jesus calls out to us,

> *"Come to me all you who labor and are heavy laden, and I will give you rest. Take My yoke upon you, and learn from me; for I am gentle and lowly in heart; and you will find rest for your souls".* —Matthew 11:28-29

This promise of rest is not established upon the uncertainties of this world but upon Christ's unshakable character and unconditional love.

Jesus said, "*I came to give life and to give it more abundantly.*" His promise is not found in keeping pace with Madison Avenue, peer pressure, or corporate America. Many of those seeking the abundant life in the midst of overwhelming deadlines, myriads of meetings, and mountains of paperwork are slowly awakening to a nagging suspicion their hope has been misplaced. Meaningful living lies beyond the office, the rush for more, or the latest craze from Apple, Amazon, or an Android app. 📖

*Be of good courage,
and He shall strengthen
your heart,
all you who hope in the
LORD*
~ Psalm 31:24 ~

Defining Hope

"Most controversies would soon be ended, if those engaged in them would first accurately define their terms, and then adhere to their definitions."
—Tryon Edwards

I pull my hefty seven-pound edition of the *American Heritage Dictionary* off an overstuffed shelf and look up the word hope. It's defined as:

1. To wish for something with expectation of its fulfillment.
2. *Archaic*: To have confidence; trust.

The dictionary lists several other definitions along with sample sentences. Obviously, the word is well defined. Our problem is not in defining hope. Our problem stems from people holding various, and at times erroneous, ideas

> Essentially there are four views on hope.

about the essence of genuine hope for a hurried world. There are four essential views on hope. Yet only one brings real meaning to life along with a lasting serenity in a world running headlong into an unknown future.

A FUTILE HOPE:

Years ago, as the story goes, a Native American boy found an eagle's egg that had fallen from its nest. Unable to replace it, he did what he thought was the next best thing. He placed it underneath a prairie chicken. Predictably, the hen sat on the egg along with her own. In time all the eggs hatched, including the eaglet. Naturally the eaglet mimicked the behavior of the prairie chickens. It scratched for seeds and insects to eat and only briefly flew a few feet off the ground. The eagle lived its life as a prairie chicken. Years passed. One day the eagle managed to see a magnificent bird high up in the cloudless sky. It soared effortless upon the wind to the amazement of the old eagle.

"What a beautiful bird," remarked the eagle to one of the chickens nearby. "What is it?"

"That's an eagle—the greatest of all birds," replied the prairie chicken. "But you'll never be like him. Don't even give it a second thought."

So the adopted eagle never gave it a second thought and died thinking it was a prairie chicken.

The Futilist views life much like the old eagle; failing to believe he can happily soar on the wings of living hope. He looks no further than present circumstances. For the most part he holds no expectations of ever finding lasting peace or real happiness in a world racing by at NASCAR speeds.

Many who fall into this line of thinking are self-proclaimed materialists; readily confessing the meaning of life is confined to their five senses. For them, the notion of finding rest for the soul within spiritual realities borders on the absurd. They typically deny the dogma of special creation. Placing one's hope in God is foreign to their way of thinking. Shunning the supernatural, they believe the world is in the death grip of random chance. Of those who may admit God exists, they view Him as distant and uninvolved in anyone's personal life, or perhaps powerless to affect any positive changes in our world. For the Futilist, life holds no certainties except the proverbial death and taxes.

Such a bleak outlook on life strikes the same chord as expressed by King Solomon in the book of Ecclesiastes. Known for his great wisdom Solomon states his own futility in trying to find gratification and meaningful living apart from God. The pursuit of his objectives without God carried him into the realms of sexual pleasure, excessive drinking, construction projects, cultivation of orchards, amassing wealth and multiplying servants and wives—none of which he discovered satisfied his soul.

His endeavors only led him to ask, "What's the point?" Is it any wonder he declared time and again, "Vanity of vanities, all is vanity." His deliberate efforts to find fulfillment were, he concluded, fruitless. In the end, life was pointless. That is, until he looked up. And there he saw his

> Vanity of vanities, all is vanity.

Creator. His outlook promptly changed. Life's meaning suddenly sharpened into focus. This king turned philosopher finally understood that life's true value is tied to the eternal—tied to God. Solomon saw the Lord as the missing element in his search for contentment and meaning. He understood at long last that God alone is that missing piece of the puzzle.

Working through his long string of self-imposed explorations of the soul, Solomon discovered life without God is an empty existence at best. As a result, he councils his readers: "Remember now your Creator in the days of your youth."[9] His entire experience is summed up in the final verses of Ecclesiastes: "Let us hear the conclusion of the whole matter: Fear God and keep His commandments…"[10]

Those same feelings of futility experienced by Solomon still live today. Multitudes find their endeavors offer, at best, short-term gratification. Restless hearts are still yearning for peace while other troubled souls still question the long-term value of all their efforts and hard work.

On January 8, 1956, Elisabeth Elliot lost her husband to Christian martyrdom. Jim Elliot died at the hands of the Auca Indians in Ecuador, along with fellow missionaries, Ed McCully, Roger Youderian, Pete Fleming, and pilot, Nate Saint.

After making first contact with the native Indians, Elliot and his partners built a base camp a short distance from their village. The Auca were widely known for their savagery. Nevertheless, encouraged by the initial friendliness of the Indians the men planned a visit to the tribal village the next day. Sadly that night a group of tribesmen emerged from the jungle and killed Elliot and his four companions. At first their efforts to evangelize the Auca appeared futile. But a few of the widowed wives and children built upon the foundation laid by their husbands and eventually saw many of the Auca come to Christ, including several of the men who took part in the killings. In her book *Keep A Quiet Heart*, Elisabeth Elliot, having experienced the tragedy of widowhood at a young age writes:

> Some of you are perhaps feeling that you are voyaging just now on a moonless sea. Uncertainty surrounds you. There seem to be no signs to follow. Perhaps you feel about to be engulfed by loneliness...[11]

Her words strike home for many of us. There are times when life's "uncertainty surrounds" us and we find ourselves sailing on a "moonless sea." Rather than finding a meaningful destination we seem to be running in circles. Our efforts to satisfy the longings of our heart remain at bay. Yet we push ahead by sheer endurance. Like Solomon, we continue to search for answers. In the end, however, Solomon found his answer.

For those like King Solomon wearied by the relentless pursuit for meaning or finding a lasting peace in a hurried world the Bible offers vibrant consolation—

> *"Those who wait on the LORD shall renew their strength; they shall mount up with wings like eagles; they shall run and not be weary, they shall walk and not faint.*
>
> —Isaiah 40:31

To which we might add, ...and they shall find hope in a hurried world.

A QUIXOTIC HOPE:

Quixotic (kwiks-ot'ik) is an odd word. It originates from the impractical hero of Cervantes' satirical novel, *Don Quixote de la Mancha*. In part quixotic means: "The pursuit of unreachable goals; idealistic without regard to practicality; apt to be deluded." Not unlike the fictional Don Quixote whose worldview was a delusion, the quixotic hopeful is somehow convinced the sun will always shine, that those rainy days of trouble will never darken their skies.

The quixotic hopeful tenaciously clings to the naïve belief that life *does* play favorites; that they are somehow immune from most, if not all, of life's unpleasant consequences. They believe if God exists at all, He is most certainly a God of love and therefore, would never allow long-term misfortune to invade their lives. In the mind of the quixotic hopeful, only others are left to experience life's worst. They are confident that with God's help any disagreeable circumstances will be short-lived and always turn out well. To their way of thinking God will do for them what He may not do for others. It's a hope tied to an unrealistic expectation.

The Quixotic hopeful is much like the man who applied for the position of town deputy. The sheriff eventually called the man in for an interview. The sheriff assured him the questions were not difficult but a necessary part of the interview process.

"Okay," began the sheriff, "What is 1 and 1?"

"Eleven," replied the applicant.

The sheriff thought to himself, "That's not what I meant, but he's right."

Then the sheriff asked the prospective deputy, "What two days of the week start with the letter 'T'?"

"Today and tomorrow," replied the candidate.

The sheriff was again surprised over the answer, one that he had never thought of himself.

"Now, listen carefully, who killed Abraham Lincoln?" asked the sheriff.

The man seemed a little surprised at the question. After thinking it over for a minute he finally admitted, "I don't know."

The sheriff replied, "Well, why don't you go home and work on that one for a while?"

The would-be deputy left the interview and met up with friends who were anxious to hear the results of the interview.

"The job is mine!" beamed the man. "First day on the job and I'm already working on a murder case!"

Unrealistic in his outlook, the would-be deputy became blinded to the real outcome of the interview. He's like the man who jumps from the 80th floor of his office building and is heard yelling as he falls past the 20th floor, "I'm still okay!"

For the quixotic hopeful misfortune only strikes others. Reality of course teaches us otherwise. Hardships *do* cross our path. Troubles *will* find us. Health problems *will* arise.

In a world far from perfect, adverse circumstances do take up permanent residence. We are painfully aware that some stroke victims do remain paralyzed—unresponsive to physical therapy. Some autistic children will never effectively function at the dizzying pace of our hurried world. And for many others, lifelong dreams will never be realized.

When such realities hit home, the quixotic optimist is forced to question their long-held assurances that tragedy would never touch their lives. Those who hold religious beliefs may begin to question their own faith or the sincerity of God's love. They may go so far as to deny the value of spiritual truths or be plagued by other spiritual concerns regarding a God they assumed would never let them down. When forced to live with the harsh realities of this world a quixotic hope withers and dies.

Optimism is strongly tied to the idealism of youth. Though optimism is no respecter of age, generally speaking those who are young tend to live with the impression that health, beauty, energy, and strength will never fade. From their youthful perspective adversity will never touch their lives. Naturally, the passing years reveal the distressing reality that strength does wane, beauty does fade, plans do fail, relationships can fall apart, and health can be broken. Painfully they learn that life does not play favorites. Their exaggerated optimism is eventually tempered by sensibility and maturity.

In the real world, trouble comes straight at us. It invades our lives by poor health, broken homes, or broken finances. Thousands live under the stress of a strained marriage or divorce. If children are involved the struggle is only compounded. Friendships and families can be shattered through pride and anger. Much can, and does, go wrong in this world. Unquestionably our need is for a living hope that offers peace of heart and mind in the midst of life's unrelenting storms.

THE HOPE OF OPTIMISM:

Did you hear about the optimistic little leaguer? It seems he was sitting in the team dugout when a man arriving after the start of the game asked the boy the score.

"Eighteen to nothing—we're behind," said the youngster.

"Wow," remarked the man, "you must be discouraged."

"Why should I be discouraged?" replied the

boy. "We haven't even gotten up to bat yet."

Like most, this youngster possessed a good deal of optimism. It doesn't take much imagination to realize how unbearable life would be without some degree of hopefulness. It's the psychological elixir that strengthens the fainting spirit and lifts the faltering heart. The extraordinary power of optimism dramatically improves one's outlook when bound by less-than-desirable circumstances.

We're reminded of the cheerful airline pilot who announced, "Good afternoon, ladies and gentlemen. We hope you're enjoying your flight. I have some good news and some bad news. The bad news is that we're flying at thirty-six thousand feet in a dense cloud formation, hopelessly lost. The good news is that we're twenty minutes ahead of schedule." Now that's optimism.

Good mental health depends on a generous dose of optimism. Medical studies have shown the enormous benefits of an optimistic outlook for healing or for those facing long recoveries. Such a state of mind has the power to effect physiological changes for the better.

Optimism typically holds a hope for a better future. It's first cousin to wishful thinking that most problems will be solved; and given enough time, money, and human ingenuity illnesses can be cured and strident hardships overcome.

Considering the medical advancements we've made over the last century, robust optimism, hard work, and ingenuity have accomplished the near miraculous. Optimism landed Neal Armstrong on the moon in 1969. It has climbed Mt. Everest, searched the depths of the ocean, and saved animals from extinction. Optimism has rescued addicts from the streets, fed the hungry, and housed the homeless. It's benefits and accomplishments are nearly limitless.

And yet hope tied solely to the power of optimism is a fragile flame at best. A single incident of long-term or permanent misfortune can extinguish its encouraging glow.

On a hot July in 1967, Joni Eareckson dove into the shallow waters of the Chesapeake Bay. Her life was forever changed in that single act of youthful enthusiasm. Striking her head on a submerged rock, Joni was instantly paralyzed from the neck down. What came next was a long emotional journey through despair, anguish, and thoughts of suicide, all now highlighted in her autobiography *Joni, an Unforgettable Story*.

From the outset her abiding Christian faith led her to believe that God would heal her body. Her hope was based on a miracle. It never came. Yet in the midst of Joni's doubts and fears God had not abandoned her. Instead, through agonizing weeks, months, and years God graciously matured her faith. Eventually she came to understand that hope must be placed upon the Lord Himself—not in her expectations of what He should do.

Joni recounts in her autobiography the long road traveled towards accepting her disability. She learned God would use her as a quadriplegic in a far greater capacity than she ever imagined. Happily married, Joni Eareckson-Tada became the founder and president of *Joni and Friends*, an internationally recognized organization that has a Christian outreach to the disabled community. As a result of her ordeal God uses her to benefit many others like herself. Her worldwide appearances, broadcasts, and best-selling books have reached multitudes of hurting people with words of comfort and spiritual encouragement. The road she would have never chosen to travel became God's conduit of grace and blessings to multiplied thousands.

We all recoil at the prospect of traveling the less desirable route of ill health, a broken home, or a lifestyle change due to a financial setback. Yet, these situations, and others like them, are what God uses to draw us closer to Him. In deliberate fashion, the Lord works to transform both our perspective and our attitude toward those unfavorable circumstances that we instinctively shun.

> All of us recoil at the prospect of traveling the less desirable route of ill health

When tragedy strikes, we desperately seek to have our old life back. When it fails to materialize, much like a branch cut from its root, our optimism withers, leaving us emotionally distressed. Fear and anger spring up. This was the place Joni found herself when faced with the prognosis of permanent paralysis. Ironically, her misfortune became the conduit toward a life of far deeper meaning and worth. At the same time the Lord showed Joni that He Himself was her sufficiency. In the end, her ordeal became the foundation for genuine hope.

Fortunately, most difficulties *do* improve with time; most illnesses *are* cured; most problems *are* solved. But there are instances, as in the case of Joni Eareckson-Tada, when the consequences of living in a broken world weave themselves permanently into the fabric of our lives.

The fanciful hope that things will *always* be made right by pushing harder on the accelerator of personal ambition or self-effort is, at best, wishful thinking. Hope must be something more than what the dictionary defines as a "wish for something with the expectation of its fulfillment."

A line from Alexander Pope's *Essay on Man* identifies the human capacity for optimism. He writes, "Hope springs eternal in the human breast." While this is generally true, La Rochefoucauld is far more accurate when he writes: "Hope, deceitful as it is, serves at least to lead us to the end of life along an agreeable road."

Hope indeed can make life's journey more "agreeable." But a hope based solely on wishful thinking is, as La Rochefoucauld put it, "deceitful." For the first thing it promises more than it can deliver. Many have found out that wishful thinking doesn't automatically make the grass greener on the other side. Many have found this out after jumping the fence for greener pastures. Wishful thinking betrays us emotionally when things don't turn out as we "hoped."

Wishful thinking is also deceitful when its anticipated end never comes to fruition. At which point frustration sets in, dragging along her siblings of discouragement and despair.

In the end, optimism born of wishful thinking is hope of a baser sort. It cannot deliver a comfort that speaks to the heart when overwhelming circumstances come to live with you. Neither does such thinking provide answers to those questions that first jump from our lips when our hurried world brings trouble: "Why" and "How long?"

The earlier journal entry accurately describes a wishful hope:

> At a distance maybe faith…Maybe we are moving in the right direction.

With their world (and their emotions) coming apart at the seams, this family holds to little more than wishful optimism. Without any real assurances they can only say, *"maybe faith…Maybe we are moving in the right direction.* Unsure that circumstances were moving in the "right direction" there is little conviction behind their words. With only a "maybe" as their hope you sense their yearning for a hope that cannot be pulled from its mooring in the midst of life's storm; an enduring hope that replaces their "maybe" with a certainty that only comes through unshakable faith standing upon a solid foundation.

For many career-minded individuals the "agreeable road" has ended with acute disappointment. Having reached the top of their profession, they're suddenly faced with the stark reality that happiness and contentment were not waiting for them—that elusive piece of life's puzzle remains stubbornly missing.

By experiencing tragedy firsthand some have lost hope by refusing to believe a loving God would allow their suffering to continue unabated. Divorced from the last vestiges of expectation their emotions are drained. Others have found the golden years tarnished beyond recognition by waning health or financial woes, forcing them to question the basis of their hope.

Fear rides upon misfortune. It's an insufferable emotion and cruel taskmaster. Fear raises its ugly head when uncertainty crosses our path. Peace evaporates like the morning dew. And yet, strangely enough, fear can be a blessing in disguise for those searching for genuine hope.

John Calvin, the sixteenth century protestant reformer, explains this bond between hope and fear:

> Fear and hope may seem opposite and incompatible affections; yet it is proved by observation that the latter never comes into full sway unless there exists some measure of

the former. In a tranquil state of mind there is no scope for the exercise of hope. David feared, and yet trusted; was sensible of the greatness of his danger, and yet quieted his mind with the confident hope of the divine deliverance.

Calvin is referring above to the fearful time in King David's life by threats of death from his enemies. Yet David resolutely declared,

"Why are you cast down, O my soul? And why are you disquieted within me? Hope in God..." — Psalm 42:5

Are you grappling with fear in your life? Has misfortune recently crossed your path? Are you trying to move on from a broken relationship yet feel God has let you down? Be assured, He has not. It is not in God's nature to let people down. His desire is for us to settle our hope, not on an ever-changing world or wishful thinking, but rather upon Him alone.

Years ago a renowned Scottish preacher affirmed, "The most profane word we use is hopeless. When you say a situation or a person is hopeless, you are slamming the door in the face of God."

The benefits of optimism are immeasurable, but they only go so far. A world teaming with uncertainties necessitates the need to venture one step further and firmly lay hold on a living, tangible hope, the source of which is God Himself.

He is the anchor that firmly secures us against the ever-shifting tides on life's stormy seas.

A GENUINE, LIVING HOPE

When God becomes the object of our hope we are finally standing on solid ground. Author Randy Alcorn makes the vital connection between real hope and God. In his book, *Heaven*, he writes:

> Secular optimists are wishful thinkers. Discovering the present payoffs of optimism they conduct seminars and write books on thinking positively. Sometimes they capitalize on optimism by becoming rich and famous. But then what happens? They eventually get old or sick, and when they die they go to Hell forever. Their optimism is an illusion, for it fails to take eternity into account.
>
> The only proper foundation for optimism is the redemptive work of Jesus Christ. Any other foundation is sand, not rock. It will not bear the weight of our eternity.[12]

Again consulting my weighty dictionary, I find the "archaic" definition for the word *hope* is, "to have confidence; trust." The question then becomes: In whom or what do we place our confidence or trust?

In John 14:1 Jesus, speaking with His disciples on the night of His betrayal, declared, "Let not your heart be troubled; you believe in God, believe also in Me." Most of us believe in God, but fewer believe in Jesus as their Lord and Savior. Is your trust in Jesus Christ as your means of salvation…as your means for peace and contentment in this hurried world?

It's clear that a living hope must be found in the divine. Anything else falls short of holding up in a world of hurry.

> Most people use the word *hope* as a synonym for wish, or want, or desire. In other words, they say, "I hope So-and-so comes...I hope I get the job I'm seeking...I hope I get the grades I'm pursuing...I hope I get accepted here or accepted there...I hope that my dream for this comes to pass." And it's nothing more than an expression of a wish.
>
> That is not the way the Bible uses the word hope. In the Bible the word hope is not a wish, it is not a fantasy, it is not a dream, it is not an allusion, it is not a plan that someone works out, it is a reality. It is a fact not yet realized. But it is nonetheless a fact and nonetheless a reality. It is just not yet realized. So when we talk about hope we're talking about something that is true, factual, promised by God and will come to pass.[13]

One artist illustrates this notion of living hope through his painting of a burned-out mountain cabin. All that remains is the stone chimney. Charred debris of what once were the family's possessions lay strewn in the foreground. A grandfather dressed only in his long johns stands in front of the destroyed cabin with his young grandson who's clutching a pair of patched overalls. The boy is crying. Inscribed beneath the picture are the heartfelt words of the old man comforting his grandson. They are both profound and poignant: "Hush child, God ain't dead."

Like the grandfather we need to clutch to a bold confidence that, "God ain't dead" when tragedy strikes. Armed with such reality life becomes a hope-filled journey rather than a frightful passage. Actively involving God in our lives is a far better alternative than building hope upon wishful thinking. The serenity we seek is found in knowing God can be trusted in our darkest hours.

A number of years ago, Warren Wiersbe, then senior pastor of the Moody Church in Chicago, presented a series of radio messages on encouragement entitled, "Songs in the Night." Later gathered into a small volume entitled *Bumps Are What You Climb On*, one message clearly identifies the firm foundation upon which living hope stands:

> When you know Jesus Christ, you always have hope. Paul tells us that Jesus Christ is our hope. To the Christian, hope is not a mirage or a blind optimism. Our hope in Christ is a certainty. Hebrews 6:19 tell us that our hope in Christ is an anchor. And that anchor will never slip or never fail. The Christian 'rejoices in hope' because he knows that the future is secure in Christ.

> Our hope in Christ is based on the Word of God, the Bible. Because we trust His promises, we experience His hope. No matter how dark the day may become, we still have the light of His Word to encourage us. Ferdinand Magellan took thirty-five compasses with him while he started on his voyage around the world. A ship without a compass is doomed—and so is a life without hope. The Word of God is the light that encourages us and the compass that guides us."[14]

The "compass" of God's Word not only guides us, it clearly points to Christ as the Way. The Bible likens Jesus to a Rock, a Foundation, and a Cornerstone. In each case the implication is clear. A hope placed in Christ offers a confidence established upon the solid assurance of His character and the worth of His person. But the basis for our confidence in Him does not end there.

Christ is eternal. As such, our reliance upon Him is a hope settled upon the eternal, not upon a temporal world with its shifting values and circumstances. A living hope is secure enough to weather the tensions of a time-pressed world caught in the rat race of hurry. If we embrace such hope that's found in Christ alone it will one day carry us beyond life's troubling storms into the very presence of our Creator.

The Truth Behind Living Hope

And you shall know the truth, and the truth shall make you free. — *John 8:32*

Jesus said unto him, "I am the way, the truth, and the life. No one comes to the Father except through me." — *John 14:6*

Christ declared, "I am...the truth." Arguably this is one of the most hotly debated assertions of the last two millennia.

Agreeing on truth has always been difficult due to the vast difference of opinions regarding how, exactly, truth can be determined and where it's to be found. A wide number of viewpoints confront us here. Is truth merely metaphysical? Is it relative? Is it only found by scientific investigation? Is it based strictly on observation? Does truth only encompass the physical world? Can truth be found in religion? And if so, which one? If we settle upon a single religious belief as a basis of truth there yet remains the daunting task of sorting through a myriad of philosophical nuances of that religion—differences based on cultural backgrounds, personal opinions and interpretations. In the case of most religions we're also faced with a menagerie of creeds or a host of denominational differences. Is it any wonder such confusion exists regarding the person of Jesus Christ or the validity of the Bible as the source of truth.

Despite the wide diversity of beliefs, human philosophies, and religious convictions there is one unifying factor—everyone agrees genuine hope must be linked to truth. No one would knowingly embrace a deception on which to pin his or her hope. Getting to the heart of the matter is simply this: who is right when it comes to truth?

To answer that question we must ask ourselves does the "truth" we hold lead to an unwavering hope? That is, does it offer a hope that will stand up to the severest of circumstances? Is our hope viable in the cultural West and well as the Far East? Is it

> Does the "truth" we hold lead to an unwavering hope?

relevant at any point in human history? Is it equally adequate for both the ancient world as well as the post-modern world? In other words, is it a hope for the ages?

Not only that, does our hope—and the truth from which it stems—work to meet mankind's greatest needs? Does it offer answers for those asking, "Why," in their broken and hurting world? Does it assist the helpless? Does it offer rest in a restless world? Most importantly, will it carry us without fear into eternity? The good news is that such hope *can* be found by setting aside prejudices and preconceptions, and boldly stepping onto the pages of Scripture. There we come face-to-face with both truth and the living hope it provides.

Understandably, not everyone agrees. Many are intolerant of the suggestion that truth, and thus real hope, is centered in the Bible at all—much less in Jesus Christ. Their claim is that hope can be settled upon any number of ideologies or religious philosophies—or even in no religion at all. To their way of thinking, the source of one's hope is simply a question of personal perspective or belief. In other words, one conviction is as good as the next. In their eyes truth is relative. Yet such an approach to defining truth produces an untenable position.

Christian apologist Dr. Norman Geisler points out the error of such thinking,

> If relativism were true, then the world would be full of contradictory conditions. For if something is true for me but false for you, then opposite conditions exist. For if I say 'There is milk in the refrigerator' and you say 'there is not any milk in the refrigerator'—and we're both right, then there must both be and not be milk in the refrigerator at the same time in the same sense. So, if truth were relative, then an impossible would be actual. [15]

As Geisler explains, a confirmed fact cannot support the possibility of an opposing "fact." Truth cannot contain a contradiction. Only a single reality is possible in any given area of inquiry, whether it's science, music, sports, or religion. Truth is based on facts—not on someone's particular belief or conviction.

We must determine then, what exactly, is the available evidence if we're expected to conclude the Bible, along with its inherent promises, is indeed *the* truth? Or to put it another way, what facts support both the validity of Christ's claims and the Bible's accuracy? For the sake of space we'll simply note the following:

1) **Manuscript evidence** has proven the Bible to be the most accurately copied volume of all ancient books. The Dead Sea scrolls, first discovered in 1947, containing mostly Hebrew texts of biblical writings, have shown modern translations of the Bible to be accurately aligned with these ancient manuscripts dating back in at least one case nearly 3,000 years. One time director for the British Museum, Sir Fredric Kenyon concludes, "The last foundation for any doubt that the Scriptures came down to us as they were written has finally been removed."[16]

2) **Archeological evidence** has proved the Bible's accuracy. Over 25,000 historical sites have been excavated and studied by top archeologists over the last two centuries. Many have verified biblical references to rulers, locations, and civilizations once thought to be either non-existent or incorrectly labeled. For instance, the Hittite civilization was once thought to be a

fabrication of Old Testament writers until 20th century archeological discoveries confirmed its existence.

3) **Historical evidence** has shown the reliability of the Bible. Through their continued efforts, modern historians have identified empires, rulers, and prominent historical figures, along with scores of past events—all of which are accurately named in the Bible.

4) **Prophetic evidence** substantiates the accuracy of the Bible. No religious book on earth contains such exacting prophecy as the Bible. The fanfare over Nostradamus and his book of prophecies, *Centuries*, written in 1555 is without warrant. His prophecies are vague passages that can easily be interpreted in any number of ways. The Bible is decidedly different. Its prophecies name specific places, people, and events. Take, for example, the Old Testament prophecy naming Christ's birthplace as the town of Bethlehem 700 years before the actual event (Micah 5:2), or Cyrus, king of the Medo-Persian Empire named nearly 150 years before his reign.

We also find specific lengths of time prophetically referenced, as in the case of Israel being in Egypt for 400 years (Gen.15:13), or the prophecy of Israel's return from the Babylonian captivity after 70 years (Jer.25:11; 29:10). There's no room for doubt. Of all the prophecies given in Scripture, upwards of 2,000 have already come to pass and have done so within the impossibly narrow (miraculous) parameters of those specific details as revealed in the Bible.

5) **Scientific evidence** attests to the Bible's veracity in revealing what otherwise could not be known at the time of the writing. For instance, in the book of Job we are told God "hangs the earth upon nothing" (Job 26:7). Written nearly 4,000 years ago, the law of gravity, let alone its force upon our planet, was the furthest thing from anyone's mind, including Job's. Modern science, far from disproving scientific references and statements in the Bible, only substantiates them.

An honest assessment of historical accounts, archeological and scientific evidences, as well as personal testimonies, all bring to light the authenticity of the Bible's claims. The indisputable veracity of the Bible leaves little room for debate regarding Jesus' emphatic declaration: "I am the way, the truth, and the life" (John 14:6).

For those who remain skeptical, one historical event offers an undeniable proof: the resurrection of Jesus Christ. His tomb is empty! This alone confirms the Gospel accounts. Following Jesus' death, no one was able to produce the body. Certainly the Romans soldiers guarding His tomb would have come up with Jesus' body in an effort to save their own skins. And being paid by the

Jewish leadership to claim the body was stolen only proves the need for an alibi. If able, the religious elite would have gladly produced the body to squelch the spreading proclamation of Jesus' resurrection.

And if, as was supposed, the disciples had actually taken Christ's body then we are faced with an insurmountable dilemma. These men had willingly sacrificed their lives for what they knew to be a falsehood regarding the resurrection. Moreover without the proof of the resurrection they died a martyr's death for a man who lied about being Israel's Messiah and the Son of God.

McDowell cites the following comment by literary English skeptic turned Christian, Frank Morison (1881-1950), author of *Who Moved the Stone?*

> In all the fragments and echoes of this far-off controversy which have come down to us, we are nowhere told that any responsible person asserted that the body of Jesus was still in the tomb. We are only given reasons why it was not there. Running all through these ancient documents is the persistent assumption that the tomb of Christ was vacant. Can we fly in the face of this cumulative and mutually corroborative evidence? Personally, I do not think we can. The sequence of coincidences is too strong.[17]

The resurrection is incontestable proof of the deity of Jesus Christ and His power over death itself. Christian apologist and author, Francis A. Schaeffer, makes the argument in his book, *The God Who is There*, of the integral relationship between truth, hope, and the resurrection:

> Christianity is realistic because it says that if there is no truth, there is also no hope; and there can be no truth if there is no adequate base. [Truth] is prepared to face the consequences of being proved false and say with Paul: "If you find the body of Christ, the discussion is finished; let us eat and drink, for tomorrow we die."[18]

The Bible clearly testifies, Christ "presented Himself alive after his suffering by *many infallible proofs*…" (Acts 1:2). A hope therefore centered in the living Lord, by "infallible proofs" is a living hope indeed. It cannot be trampled underfoot by life's harsh realities or outpaced by a world of hectic hurry.

გაი

Now, faith is one thing, and hope is another. When hope takes the place of faith, it is a snare. Faith is to work and trust...but hope is to wait and trust; to wait and expect; in other words, that hope is the daughter of faith. I heard a very godly man once say that joy was like the larks, that sang in the morning when it was light, but hope was like the nightingale, that sang in the dark; so that hope was really better than joy.

— Dwight L. Moody

Hope...is not...a form of escapism or wishful thinking, but one of the things a Christian is meant to do. It does not mean that we are to leave the present world as it is. If you read history, you will find that the Christians who did the most for the present world were just those who thought most of the next...Aim at Heaven and you will get Earth thrown in: aim at Earth and you will get neither.

— C.S. Lewis, *Mere Christianity*

Types of Hope
Found in the Bible

Living .... **I Peter 1:3**
Blessed be the God and Father of our Lord Jesus Christ, Who according to His abundant mercy has begotten us again to **a living hope** through the resurrection of Jesus Christ from the dead. 📖

Blessed .... **Titus 2:13**
Looking for the **blessed hope**, and glorious appearing of our great God and our Savior Jesus Christ. 📖

Good .... **II Thessalonians 2:16,17**
Now may our Lord Jesus Christ Himself, and our God and Father, who has loved us and given us everlasting consolation and **good hope** by grace, comfort your hearts, and establish you in every good word and work. 📖

Better .... **Hebrews 7:19**
For the law made nothing perfect; on the other hand, there is the bringing in of a **better hope**, through which we draw near to God. 📖

Sure & Steadfast .... **Hebrews 6:19**
This **hope** we have as an anchor of the soul, both **sure and steadfast**... 📖

What Has Science to Say?

"Today, many have hijacked science, insisting that it can only be done within an atheistic frame of reference (or worldview), thus completely removing God from our thinking about the physical world." —Roger Patterson

The famous Congregational preacher Joseph Parker (1830-1902) once delivered a sermon about living hope. A hope not found in science but in the Bible. He concluded his message by saying, "Some have found fault with me. They say I am old-fashioned and out of date...I am always quoting the Bible...why not turn to science this morning?

"There is a poor widow here who has lost her only son. She wants to know if she will see him again. Science shall give the answer, and I will put the Book away." At this point Parker placed the Bible he was holding on the seat behind him, then continued to speak. "Will this woman see her son again? Where is he? Does death end all? What has science to say?" Here he gave a long pause. "We are waiting for an answer, the woman is anxious." Another long pause. "The woman's heart is breaking. Science must speak. Nothing to say?

Surely?

"Then we must take the Book," and here Joseph Parker reverently took the Bible up again and opened it and read: "I shall go to him, but he shall not return to me...the dead shall rise...for this corruptible must put on incorruption, and this mortal must put on immortality. O death, where is thy sting... I saw the dead, small and great stand before God."

Closing the Bible, and patting it affectionately, Parker said, "We will stick to the Book."

༺༻

Hope is nothing else than the expectation of the things that faith has believed to be truly promised by God.

~ John Calvin ~

༺༻

"*I* have hoped in Your Word"
—*Psalm 119:74*

Hope in God
And now Lord, what do I wait for? **My *hope* is in You**. — *Psalm 39:7*

Hope in Christ
If in this life only we have *hope* **in Christ**, we are of all men most pitiable. —*I Corinthians 15:19*

Hope of Eternal Life
That having been justified by His grace we should become heirs according to the *hope* **of eternal life**.

—*Titus 3:7*

Hope in the Scriptures
For whatever things were written before were written for our learning, that we **through patience and comfort of the Scriptures** might have *hope*.

—*Romans 15:4*

Hope in Christ's Return
Looking for the blessed *hope* and glorious appearing of our great God and Savior Jesus Christ.

—*Titus 2:13*

The Bible is a Book of Hope

"...Seek and you will find;
knock, and it will be opened to you."
— *Luke 11:9*

During his long years in Russian prisons and work camps as a political dissident Anatoli Shcharansky was stripped of all his personal belongings. Only a miniature copy of the Psalms remained. Once during his imprisonment his refusal to release the book to the authorities cost him 130 days in solitary confinement. After twelve years of imprisonment, he was finally given his freedom. In February 1986, the world watched as Shcharansky walked past the Russian guards toward those who would take him to Jerusalem and his wife. But in the final moments of captivity, the guards tried again to confiscate his book of Psalms. Anatoli threw himself face down and refused to walk on to freedom without it. Those words of encouragement and promises of God had kept him alive during his imprisonment. He refused freedom without them.

Down through the centuries multitudes have found their refuge and strength within the Bible. To this day, it remains the lifeblood of vital hope for multiple thousands around the world. Naysayers remain skeptical, arguing the Scriptures are unable to meet the needs of a modern world. Others erroneously believe the Bible only offers a "sweet by and by" hope. But an honest evaluation of the world's best selling book silences its critics. Its pages contain promises relevant to life—yes, even the hectic, near-crazed pace of living in our twenty-first century.

God's promises aren't limited to only a hope for heaven and a future resurrection. They encompass a vital hope for living in the here-and-now. The God of the Bible is a God of love. He sees and knows our pains, our troubles, and our frustrations. He understands our daily challenges. In His great mercy and grace He supplies a down-to-earth, rubber-meets-the-road hope for the battles we face. Do you need some encouragement and a fresh anointing of hope? You need travel no further than the Bible. It is filled with promises for the world-weary, as well as accounts of those who placed their hope in the Lord and thereby gained the encouragement and comfort they needed. Search out God's promises and those accounts of trust for yourself. You'll find a wealth of strength and hope to combat our world of stress.

※

Behind the cloud the starlight lurks,
Through showers the sunbeams fall;
For God, who loveth all his works,
Has left his hope with all.

—Whittier: *Dream of Summer*—

※

A Quick Study on Hope

> For whatever things were written before were written for our learning, that we through patience and comfort of the Scriptures might have hope.
> — *Romans 15:4*

Three truths immediately jump out from our verse above. To begin with we find the Bible (specifically the Old Testament in the context of this verse) was written for "our learning."

TRUTH #1

If we expect any of our endeavors to succeed there must first be a learning process—a time of instruction. More importantly such instruction must come from the right source.

Obviously any successful airline pilot routinely lands safely. But such pilots acquire their skill of flying—and landing—through a training process that is suited to their profession. Let's face it, a licensed carpenter would not be competent behind the flight controls of a jetliner for the simple reason he lacks the proper training. Neither would our carpenter do well as a surgeon. While he may be skilled with saws of all sorts I'm sure none of us would want a hip replacement by him.

This principle of obtaining proper instruction is no less true with regard to hope. To embrace its genuine essence we must, of necessity, be suitably instructed.

At its very core, living hope springs from the unchangeable promises, principles, and wisdom of the eternal God. Real hope for serenity and meaningful living is conceived by spiritual instruction (Ps.32:8,9). Then, like a newborn baby, it continues to mature and grow as we apply spiritual truths to our lives (Jam.1:22).

Knowledge is the foundation for success in any endeavor, but we must build upon that foundation with hands-on application to realize success. Need proof? Try flying with a pilot whose only *read* about landing a jet. And few would take their chances with a doctor who's only watched a video on heart surgery. In much the same way, a hope that endures the thickest of times gains its strength through a hands-on application of putting spiritual principles into practice. Only then does hope take on the breath of life and provide a vital difference in our lives.

TRUTH #2

Continuing in Romans 15:4, we notice hope is derived through "patience...of the Scriptures." Our fast-paced world cruelly tears into the fabric of our lives, often exposing our impatience with trying circumstances.

Some years back I found myself in a slow-moving checkout line at Walmart. The sluggish pace was visibly frustrating everyone in line. A man somewhere behind me started complaining about the obvious lack of progress. Evidently his patience had run out. "This *is* the express line?" he questioned, hoping to grab the cashier's attention. She hears, but ignores him. We all smile. We understand how he feels. Our own growing impatience is thinly veiled behind weak smiles following the man's outburst. My own patience is not worn nearly as thin as the others in line. The reason? I made a decision years ago to never let impatience get the best of me in *any* checkout line. My secret? I focus my attention on available reading material, but mainly on my good fortune of being in a checkout line in Walmart instead of a bread line in a refugee camp. On this particular occasion I'm thumbing through a magazine borrowed off the display rack. I remain calm.

Calm tolerance in a slow moving checkout line however is not to be confused for Biblical patience. There is a time and place for controlling personal agitation, but this is not what God has in mind when He speaks of patience that undergirds living hope. The patience that supports hope is nowhere defined as short-term. Rather, it is a conviction to trust God implicitly regardless of our circumstances or the extent of time involved—including, if need be, to the end of our days.

The biblical patriarch Abraham and his wife

Sarah are prime examples of such patience. Oddly enough, this couple "died in faith, not having received the promises, but having seen them afar off were assured of them, embraced them and confessed that they were strangers and pilgrims on the earth" (Heb.11:13). For this couple, biblical patience was built upon the surety of God's promises though they would not live to see them.

Biblical patience is foundational to living hope. When patience fails, hope withers and dies. Many have planted their roots in the philosophies of this world only to witness the once fertile soil of their temporal hope dry and crack under the grueling sun of life's concerns and disappointments. On the other hand a person whose hope is rooted in God finds a fountain of living water that quenches the thirsty soul and revitalizes our faith.

> Biblical patience is foundational to living hope.

While God is able to provide immediate relief from our burdens, He may lead for us down the longer road of personal difficulties. In this way we gain patience, grow spiritually, and develop a deeper trust in Him.

The Old Testament patriarch Job embodies God's "longer road" approach of spiritual instruction. To our initial horror, the Lord allows this wealthy man to lose all of his earthly possessions. As if that wasn't enough, we're further shocked to discover Job's children are killed by invaders. Then Job's health is broken and his wife, in a fit of consternation, tells him to, "Curse God and die." Yet following this long and dark ordeal, the Lord blesses Job by restoring both his health and wealth. He's further blessed with ten additional children. The lesson is simple. God rewards spiritual patience borne of faith.

The Lord's intended lesson on patience for you and I might well be through adversity, as it was for Job:

> *My brethren, take the prophets, who spoke in the name of the Lord, as an example of suffering and patience. Indeed we count them blessed who endure. You have heard of the perseverance of Job and seen the end intended by the Lord—that the Lord is very compassionate and merciful.* —James 5:10,11

Biblical hope does not rest upon the assumption that God is obligated to deliver immediate escape from our difficulties; neither is He obliged to bend His will to ours. Yes, occasionally the Lord works a miracle in our favor, but more often He allows us to walk the longer road of spiritual growth. As such, hope cannot rest upon seeing the immediate. It must live within a framework of perseverance. In order to do so it must be settled upon the noble character of God. Hope recognizes God's ways are seldom

> ...hope cannot rest upon seeing the immediate.

instantaneous or miraculous in its fullest sense of the word. When tragedy strikes, we naturally pray for God's immediate intervention, but true hope rests contently by faith in His perfect will and His perfect timing.

Resting in such hope dispels the darkness of uncertainty; it's a hope settled on trusting God for strength to face our day-to-day challenges. Keeping a firm grip on biblical hope allows us to confidently "walk through the valley" if that is the path of God's choosing for us.

Modern living forces us into a whirlwind of hurry. We typically expect God to work at this same feverish pace. He rarely does.

> Modern living forces us into a whirlwind of hurry.

Let's be honest. We're prone to impatience groomed by a culture that thrives on instant gratification. We expect—we want—and at times we demand things be done *now*!

I'm reminded of the impatient driver who laid on his horn when the car in front of him stalled at a light and couldn't start. After repeated tries, the driver of the stalled car walked back to the impatient man still blowing his horn. "Listen," he said. "My car won't start. Would you mind trying to start it while I sit here and lean on your horn?"

When facing those never-ending to-do lists, or those furious storms that rage against our health, our security, or our emotions we crave immediate relief. Yet God's timing is never set to our watch. He moves to the hour hand of eternity. Frustrated, we want Him to move to the sweep of the second hand.

John Bunyan (1628-1688), author of the best-selling Christian allegory *The Pilgrim's Progress*, wrote:

> Hope has a thick skin and will endure many a blow; it will put on patience as a vestment, it will wade through a sea of blood, it will endure all things if it be of the right kind, for the joy that is set before it. Hence patience is called "patience of hope," because it is hope that makes the soul exercise patience and long-suffering under the cross, until the time comes to enjoy the crown.

Let's look again at Abraham and Sarah. Having traveled to the land of Canaan, God promised this childless couple a son (Gen.12:4-7). The promise was first made when Abraham was seventy-five years old and Sarah was entering her sixty-fifth year. We assume the Lord will have to hurry if He is to keep His word. And yet He waits nearly twenty-five more years. By this time Abraham is a hundred and Sarah is ninety. Only then does their promised son Isaac finally arrive (Gen.21:2-5).

We can draw three important lessons from this account. First, that God is sovereign over every circumstance you and I will ever face. He can work miracles if He so chooses, as He did in the case of Abraham and Sarah. A second lesson learned is that the Lord always keeps His promises. It may not be today, or tomorrow, or anytime soon, but they will be kept. And finally, we learn patience and faith are greatly rewarded by the Lord.

Our aversion to long lines, being placed on hold, or our tendency to forgo saving for a purchase but instead use a credit card all show we have little patience. We recoil from any type of waiting—most especially waiting on God.

Remember Veruca Salt? That spoiled brat of Willie Wonka fame who, while touring the chocolate factory with her father, constantly demanded he indulge her every impulsive whim. Her belligerent bellowing, "I want it *now*!" sounds all too familiar, echoing out our own impatience. We are instructed to let "patience have her perfect work" (Jam.1:4). In this way we avoid being impulsive children expecting—sometimes demanding—our own way with God.

The Psalmist entreats us to...

> *Wait on the Lord; be of good courage,*
> *And He shall strengthen your heart;*
> *Wait, I say, on the Lord!"* ~ Psalm 27:14

TRUTH #3

The final truth we glean from Romans 15:4 is that spiritual "comfort" is derived directly from the Bible. Promises for the wayward soul as well as the longing heart are found within its pages. By embracing God's Word as a priceless treasure, we are freed from our misgivings about trusting our own frailties or trusting a world in constant unrest. The Bible enables us to examine the character of God up close and personal. It brings into view a hope founded upon the Almighty Creator. We are awed by His care, overwhelmed by His love, and reassured by His grace, mercy, and compassion—such attributes cannot help but become the building blocks of living hope. 📖

*God is never late,
or ever in a hurry*

Mr. William Gladstone (1809-1898), one time Prime Minister of England, was an outspoken Christian. In an interview he was asked, "What do you regard as the greatest hope for the future of the human race?" Mr. Gladstone hesitated a moment then answered, "I should say we must look for that to be the maintenance of faith in the invisible. That is the great hope of the future. It is the mainstay of civilization, and by that I mean a living faith in a personal God. After sixty years of public life I hold more strongly than ever to that conviction, deepened and strengthened by long experience, of the reality and the nearness and the personality of God."

Personal Glimpses – 1

Charles Hadden Spurgeon (1834-1892) is known as the Prince of Preachers. This 19th century pastor and author delivered his sermons to over 5,000 pressed weekly into the Metropolitan Tabernacle in London. Beside local visitors, travelers from around the world often attended his church to hear him speak. Due to Spurgeon's tremendous popularity, regular church members were sometimes asked to give up their seats to accommodate the large numbers of visitors. Uncounted thousands came to Christ under his fruitful ministry. Spurgeon was also instrumental in starting an orphanage and a college for pastors. His sermons were published weekly in newspapers worldwide.

Charles Hadden Spurgeon

The influence of C.H. Spurgeon is still felt today. Major publishers regularly reprint his sermons and books. His daily devotional volume, *Morning and Evening* remains a top seller more than a century after its original publication.

Spurgeon's popularity never intimidated him to compromise on preaching the "whole council of God" or stand against the liberal theologians of his day. When he thought it necessary, his sermons lashed out God's truth with a fiery zeal that scorched the liberal teachings of his day. His enormous popularity however did not rest in his passionate ability to defend the faith, but rather in his dynamic ability to lift the spirit of his listeners. His sermons plucked souls off the harsh road of life and brought them to the Savior. He understood his audience. His listeners were either on the road to ruin, the road of despair, or in the place of blessings and joy. It didn't matter who you were, whether rich or poor, young or old, or where you found yourself along life's journey. His appeal was for saints and sinners alike to find rest in the One who said, "Come to Me, all you who labor and are heavy laden, and I will give you rest." Listen as the Prince of Preachers speaks to us on hope—

> His sermons plucked souls off the harsh road of life and brought them to his Savior.

> Jeremiah's hope was dashed upon the jagged rocks of harsh reality. He cried out, "My strength and my hope is perished from the LORD: Remembering mine affliction and my misery, the wormwood and the gall. My soul has them still in remembrance, and is humbled in me." Undoubtedly Jeremiah was a

crushed man. Jeremiah was a prophet of God who had lost his hope for Jerusalem.

The invading hordes of Babylonians were the crushing enemies for Jeremiah. Perhaps your invading army is scorn and ridicule. Perhaps it's the advancing army of cancer consuming your body; perhaps its divorce, loss of a job, or loss of a loved one. The crushing force of the enemies of this world are unrelenting, to the point of strangling the life out of our hope. Is there a solution? Yes, a thousand times, Yes! Jeremiah gives us the answer in the very next verse (Lam. 3:21,22). "This I recall to my mind, therefore have I hope." Jeremiah, what is it you recalled to mind that awakened the sleeping hope within you? What words of comfort, what promise of God can you give to us that will lift our spirit once again to the throne of God's grace? Jeremiah remembered this:

It is of the Lord's mercies that we are not consumed, because his compassions fail not. They are new every morning: great is thy faithfulness. The Lord is my portion, saith my soul; therefore will I hope in Him.

God's compassions do not fail. God's promises do not fail. God's mercies do not fail. What blessed truths these are!

AS LONG AS...

AS LONG AS matters are really hopeful, hope is a mere flattery or platitude; it is only when everything is hopeless that hope begins to be a strength. Like all the Christian virtues, it is as unreasonable as it is indispensable.

– G. K. Chesterton

AS LONG AS sight and reason find footing in matters, there is no place for faith and hope; the abundance of human helps puts not grace to proof, but the strength of faith is in the absence of them all. A man is stronger when he goes on his feet alone, than when he stands by a grip in his infancy, or leans on a staff in his old age. The two feet of faith and hope serve us best when we are fixed on the Rock of Zion alone.

– William Struther

Personal Glimpses - 2

George Müller's (1805-1898) orphanage in Bristol, England has been an object lesson of hope and prayer for over 175 years. When Müller began to care for his orphans in 1836 he resolved to depend solely upon God. From that first year until the end of 1959 his institution received more than nine million dollars in free-will gifts — solely in answer to prayer and without ever asking for a donation. More than 17,000 orphans have been blessed because of the answered prayers of George Müller.

George Müller

George Müller's prayer life and faith are legendary, inspiring countless others to place their own trust in God. Daily Müller brought his needs, whether small and great, before the Lord with absolute assurance each need would be supplied.

Once on an Atlantic crossing, Müller's ship ran into a thick fog. The vessel slowed to a crawl inching its way mile after mile. Müller approached the captain; "I must be in Quebec on Saturday afternoon."

"Impossible," said the captain. "The fog is forcing us to a near stand-still."

"Very well," replied Müller, "If your ship cannot take me, God will find some other means. I have never broken an engagement in fifty-seven years."

"I would willingly help you if I could," said the captain. "But there's nothing anyone can do."

"There is one thing we can do. Let us go to the chartroom and pray."

"Do you know how dense the fog is?" asked the captain.

"No," was Müller's response. "My eye is not on the density of the fog but on the living God who controls every circumstance of my life."

Together the two men went to the chartroom and Müller prayed: "O Lord, if it is consistent with Thy will, please remove the fog in five minutes. You know the engagement You made for me in Quebec on Saturday. I believe it is Your will."

When he had finished, the captain was about to pray, but Müller touched him on the shoulder and told him not to do so. "First," he said, "you do not believe He will; and second, I believe He has, so there is no need for you to pray about it."

The captain looked amazed and Müller continued, "Captain, I have known my Lord for fifty-seven years, and there has never been a single day that I have failed to gain an audience with Him. Get up and open the door. You will find the fog gone."

The captain, still skeptical, opened the door. To his utter amazement the fog had disappeared.

Never be cast down by trifles. If a spider breaks his web twenty times, twenty times will he mend it again. Make up your minds to do a thing, and you will do it. Fear not if trouble comes upon you; keep up your spirits, though the day may be a dark on.

> *"Troubles never last forever;*
> *The darkest day will pass away."*

If the sun is going down, look up to the stars; if the earth is dark; keep your eyes on heaven. With God's presence and God's promise, a man or child may be cheerful.

> *"Never despair when fog's in the air,*
> *A sunshiny morning will come without warning!"*
>
> — *Anonymous*

God makes a promise —
Faith believes it,
Hope anticipates it,
Patience quietly awaits it.

Waitin' for the Chewing Gum

> [By faith Abraham] waited for a city...
> whose builder and maker is God.
> — Hebrews 11:10

Best-selling author Barbara (Spatula) Johnson lived by the motto, "Life is 10% how you make it, and 90% how you take it." Over the years her humorous writing style has been a tremendous source of encouragement for many of her readers. She easily connects with her audience, not only because of her humor, but because she is comfortable with sharing her personal struggles. She lost her father at the age of twelve. Her husband was in a near-fatal accident taking many months to recover. She lost one son in the Vietnam War. A drunk driver killed her second son. And her third son, after revealing his homosexuality, disowned the family and disappeared for eleven years. Her life's lesson on hope was forged from the fires of personal tragedy and pain.

In spite of misfortune striking time after time, Barbara Johnson firmly believed "how you take it" makes all the difference. Her perspective on hope hits home as she writes, "The cutest illustration of hope I've found is about a little boy who was standing at the foot of the escalator at a large department store, intently watching the handrail. He never took his eyes off the handrail as the escalator kept going around and around. A salesperson saw him and finally asked him if he was lost. The little fellow replied, 'Nope, I'm just waitin' for my chewing gum to come back'."

Let's be honest. Our faith in God is at times anemic compared to this boy's confidence. There's no doubt in this boy's mind his wad of gum was coming around again. He's convinced of it. Some of us are convinced too. Only in our case we're convinced God's blessings have stopped circling altogether; that they have somehow slipped away forever. What we need is a good dose of this boy's know-so assurance. It's no secret his confidence was based on one simple fact—the handrail was still circling.

> No doubt in this boy's mind his wad of gum was coming around again.

Right now, you may be in the tempest of the rat race, running ragged by trying to keep up with life's hectic pace. But as surely as that young boy's handrail kept moving, so too is God still moving in this turbulent world.

Life has a way of working things out. Many troubling situations do come to a happy end. For the Christian, however, faith goes beyond simply hoping that the pieces of our lives will somehow fall into place. God never intended life to be a haphazard sequence of events that manage to turn out right. Whatever comes our way—whether good or bad—life has its purpose. We may not fully understand the extent of God's reasoning for our personal problems, but one thing is certain—God's blessings never stop circling.

As that small boy waited for his chewing gum to come around there are times we must wait on the Lord for new blessings to surface or prayers to be answered. Remember, God's timetable is not our timetable. The prophet Isaiah reminds us that waiting on God comes with its own reward; one especially needed as we face our hurried world each day.

> *But those who wait on the Lord*
> *Shall renew their strength;*
> *They shall mount up with wings like eagles,*
> *They shall run and not be weary,*
> *They shall walk and not faint.*
> —Isaiah 40:31

Meaningful lessons on trusting the Lord take place in the classroom of life. Most especially when we're faced with personal hardships, doubts, or fears. This trio-of-trouble robs us of spiritual confidence and in turn affects our faith. Yet these same difficulties are the very avenue by which we experience firsthand God's unfailing strength to carry us over the roughest roads or through the deepest valleys. With our hope focused clearly on the Lord every hardship, doubt, or fear only leads us toward spiritual maturity and draws us closer to Him who is the source of spiritual strength vitally needed to face our troubles head on.

Trials and tribulations have a unique way of bringing the spiritual side of life sharply into focus. As such, troubles that drive us to God become a spiritual opportunity. William Cook develops this idea of seeing problems as opportunities in his book, *Success, Motivation, and the Scriptures*. He writes:

> You must force yourself into exciting new thinking in the area of problems. God doesn't know a single problem He cannot turn into an opportunity. For centuries God has been taking what man considered as a problem and turning it into an opportunity—an opportunity for Him to work a miracle...When will we see through the eyes of eternity and view problems as opportunities?

The Apostle Paul discovered this opportunity through a medical disability. On three separate occasions Paul prayed for God to remove the ailment that persistently plagued him. The Lord's response is telling. He informs Paul, *"My grace is sufficient for you: for my strength is made perfect in weakness"* (2 Cor.12:9).

God flatly denied a healing. Instead, Paul's medical ailment would be the very thing God would use to demonstrate the power of His grace. Paul quickly learned serenity comes through the grace of God, not through perfect health.

Despite feelings to the contrary, those problems we find on our doorstep provide us an opportunity to draw closer to the Shepherd of our souls. Have the winds of adversity blown into your life? Are personal struggles draining your spiritual stamina? Is a family crisis plaguing your home? Lean upon the Lord. Make His grace—His strength—your own.

Trusting God is a vital element of hope. It is especially crucial when the Lord's blessings seem as sparse as the desert sands or when troubles erupt beyond our ability to control them. A deep-seated trust in God's unchanging Word provides us the assurance that His blessings are just around the bend. Are you waiting on the Lord's blessings? Take hold of King Solomon's advice:

> *Trust in the Lord with all your heart,*
> *and lean not on your own understanding.*
> —Proverbs 3:5

Tomorrow is but a mystery. Trust the One who knows and holds the future. Every detail of all our tomorrows is firmly held in the omniscient hand of God. Out of His great love and concern the Author of each new day is asking us to trust Him.

> *You [Lord] will keep him in perfect peace,*
> *Whose mind is stayed on You,*
> *Because he trusts in You.*
> *Trust in the Lord forever.* —Isaiah 26:3,4

The Poetry of Hope

> Hope is the thing with feathers
> that perches in the soul,
> And sings the tune without the words,
> And never stops at all.
> — Emily Dickinson

Years ago I conducted a funeral service for a longtime church member. Shortly before his death he jotted down some personal expressions of hope, anticipating his family would find it following his passing. As expected his wife discovered his letter sandwiched between the pages of his Bible. She asked if I would read it as part of his eulogy. I gladly agreed. His sentiments were a testimony of his faith and a clear expression of unfailing hope in Jesus Christ. His letter ended with these words, "I smile at my loved ones and say, 'Do not cry, I am going to be with my King'."

I'm reminded of the great disparity between those possessing a living hope in Christ and those who find such hope an absurdity. This difference of conviction is no better illustrated than in the lives of Lord Byron, of authorship fame, and Adam Clarke. In the case of Lord Byron he abandoned himself to the pursuit of sexual pleasure. Yet, at the age of only 36 (shortly before his untimely death), he bares his empty soul with these words:

> "My days are in the yellow leaf,
> The flowers and fruits of love are gone;
> The worm, the canker, and the grief—
> are mine alone!"

Now compare Byron's dark sentiments to the bright outlook of Adam Clarke, a devoted Christian minister and well-published Bible expositor, who at age 84 wrote:

> "I have passed through the springtime of my life. I have withstood the heat of its summer. I have culled the fruits of fall. I am even now enduring the rigors of its winter, but at no great distance I see the approach of a new, eternal springtime. Hallelujah!"

The outlook on life between these two men could not be further apart. For Byron, hope was a distant stranger. For Clarke, hope was a living, breathing companion—a reality that faithfully steered him down life's highway. Though his final days loomed near, Clarke was assured he would soon be exiting onto a new and better road (Revelation 21:21).

For more than thirty-five years Martha Snell Nicholson composed some of the finest Christian poetry that has ever been written. Jotting down some thoughts on the coming of the Lord she once wrote:

"The best part is the blessed hope of his soon coming. How I ever lived before I grasped that wonderful truth, I do not know. How anyone lives without it these trying days I cannot imagine....I am on tiptoe with expectancy. There are no more gray days—for they're all touched with color; no more dark days—for the radiance of His coming is on the horizon; no more dull days, with glory just around the corner; and no more lonely days, with His footsteps coming ever nearer, and the thought that soon I shall see His blessed face and be forever through with pain and tears."

Final Words of Hopeful Men

Sir Michael Faraday (1791-1867) is arguably one of the greatest physicists of all time. His labors and experiments helped develop the new sciences of electricity and magnetism. Faraday was also a man of great faith in Jesus Christ. When he lay dying a journalist was granted permission to interview the famous scientist. The interview progressed as planned until the journalist questioned Faraday as to his speculations for a life after death. "Speculations!" Faraday retorted. "I know nothing about speculations. I'm resting on certainties. 'I know that my Redeemer liveth,' and because He lives. I shall live also."

William Beveridge (1637-1708) was a gifted linguist. His popularity as an Anglican pastor never diminished his personal resolutions to live only for the "kingdom of God." His basis of belief was set in the authority of the Scriptures, which set him apart from many of his peers. As an author, his writings greatly influenced Christian thinking of the day. He penned several well-received treatises including those on Church history and the Oriental languages. In July

1704, he was consecrated Bishop of St. Asaph, and died at Westminster, March 5, 1708. Once asked about his relationship with Jesus Christ he answered by saying, "Oh yes, I have known Him these forty years. Precious Savior! He is my only hope."

Michaelangelo di Lodovico Buonarroti Simoni (1475-1564). The artistry and genius of Italian Renaissance painter, sculptor, architect, poet and engineer Michelangelo is legendary. His body of work is prodigious and considered the pinnicle of artisitic human achievement. His final words are a firm testimony of his abiding hope. Near the end of his life he stated, "I die in the faith of Jesus Christ and in the firm hope of a better life."

The world dare say no more for its device than, "while I live, I hope." But the children of God can all, by virtue of a living hope exclaim, "while I expire I hope."

— Robert Leighton (1611-1684) —

No Sorrow There!

This earthly life has been fitly characterized as a pilgrimage through a vale of tears. In the language of poetry, man himself has been called a pendulum between a smile and a tear. Everything in this world is characterized by imperfection. The best people have many faults. The clearest mind only sees through a glass darkly...Every heart has its grief, every house has its skeleton, every character is marred with weakness and imperfection. And all these aimless conflicts of our minds, and unanswered longings of our hearts should lead us to rejoice the more in the divine assurance that a time is coming when night shall melt into noon, and the mystery shall be clothed with glory.

— Daniel March, D.D. (1886)

Hope Answers—Let the Years Fly!

"Away, then, with judging by what you do, or see, or feel, or are. Rise into the sphere of the things which shall be. Can you not do that? When there is no joy in the present, there is an infinite joy in the future. Do not say, 'Oh, but it is a long way off.' It is not so. Many among you are sixty, seventy, or even eighty years of age; your time for the sight of Christ in your disembodied state cannot be far away, for the thread of life is snapping.

Some of us are in middle age, but as we have already reached the average of life, we are bound to reckon that our lease is far advanced; and as so many are snatched away in their prime, we may at any moment be caught up to the land for which we hope...Let us labor to our utmost for the glory of God while we are here, for the moments flash away. Do you not recollect this time last year when autumn's ripeness was all around? It seems but the other day. You boys and girls think it a long year, but the old folks are of another opinion. We have no long years now that we are growing gray.

For me time travels so fast that its axles are hot with speed. Fear cries—Oh, for a little breathing space! But hope answers— No, let the years fly, we shall be home the sooner."

~ Charles H. Spurgeon

Three Key Truths to Living Hope

> Obedience is the key to every door.
> — George MacDonald

Stock market meltdowns, mad hatters running rogue nations, racial riots, terrorist attacks, personal hardships, and life in the fast lane all testify to the crucial need for a hope that is unyielding to outside pressures. Clearly, in such troubling times, the need is greater than ever for a hope offering personal serenity and meaningful direction while enduring the unprecedented challenges of modern living. It must provide an unshakeable assurance in a world spinning madly out of control. Such hope is found in three key truths.

KEY TRUTH #1: Realize that Life has a Purpose.

A revealing poll published several years ago indicated, "One out of five Americans feel life is meaningless."[19] This comes as no surprise considering our cultural proclivity for the theory of evolution. Modern science assumes humanity arose from a cosmic happenstance; that sometime in the distant past the primordial oceans generated non-living stings of amino acids that somehow produced a "biological burp" initiating replicating molecules, eventually morphing into cells. Not content with this particular theory for the origin of life, some scientists courageously suggest that life started through an accumulation of abnormalities in the growth of crystals like quartz.

How do intelligent people reach such questionable conclusions? Simple. The science community allows for *any* theory so long as it avoids the need for a Creator. Sadly, a majority of scientists feel that acknowledging biblical creation somehow demeans their profession or strips them of their intelligence. Ironically, some of the greatest scientific minds of the past were Bible-believing creationists, including: Blaise Pascal, Robert Boyle, Isaac Newton, Carolus Linnaeus, Michael Faraday, Louis Pasteur, and Lord Kelvin. Famed rocket engineer and pioneer of manned space flight, Werner von Braun, made this assertion:

> Manned space flight is an amazing achievement, but it has opened for mankind thus far only a tiny door for viewing the awesome reaches of space. An outlook through this peephole at the vast mysteries of the universe should only confirm our belief in the certainty of its Creator. I find it as difficult to understand a scientist who does not acknowledge the presence of a superior

rationality behind the existence of the universe as it is to comprehend a theologian who would deny the advances of science.[20]

For Von Braun and other like-minded scientists there's no discrepancy between their efforts to discover how the universe functions and a belief in God. While modern science has greatly advanced our understanding of the world, it has nevertheless strayed from a belief in the supernatural. Today's science community has crossed the line of explaining how nature functions (true science) to postulating a creation devoid of a Creator.

A host of theories have risen in recent years explaining the origin of the universe and how it functions, including: parallel universes, the fractal theory, the inflationary theory, and the string theory that strives to compile all known fundamental forces and matter into a single mathematical equation, and of course the big bang theory, which promotes the idea that out of nothing exploded the fabric of space and time, including the required quantity of plasma to produce all matter now filling a universe of nearly infinite proportions with countless billions of galaxies. Plainly, none of these theories offer real meaning to life. Instead, they lead us away from the very foundation for a meaningful existence, that is, a belief that declares, "In the beginning God created the heavens and the earth."

One would have to turn a blind eye to miss the obvious correlation existing between a world created by random chance and a meaningless life. An inherit fatalism resides in the Darwinian view that deems humanity as nothing more than a fluke of nature. Humans are far more than an amalgamation of carbon compounds evolving over millions of years. We are a special creation designed to connect with our Creator.

> An inherit fatalism resides in the Darwinian view that deems humanity…a fluke of nature.

The design of living organisms at any level gives us pause for wonder. The simplest cell reveals a complexity that was hard to imagine until recently. It was once thought cells comprised of little more than an outer membrane and nucleus for replication. Crude microscopes, unable to peer into the complex interior of a cell, observed little more than what was then labeled as a "black box." Scientists have since learned living cells are highly complex organisms. Cells within the human body utilize a highly compartmentalized design, each carrying out its specific role and needing its own set of proteins to properly function. Such a complex design points directly to the Great Designer.

Evolution offers nothing more than a world of chaos and misfortune. Accepting biblical creation is to accept that life springs from God's eternal purposes and reasoning. Acceptance of the supernatural dispels the notion of a meaningless existence. Belief in God is the very heartbeat of life with meaning.

Human kind is the apex of creation. Formed in the very image of God (Gen. 1:26), men and women are uniquely diverse from the animal kingdom—a uniqueness that equates into life holding a distinct purpose. In allowing for a Creator one concedes there is a rationale behind our existence. As such, the meaning of life is infinitely more than a compilation of human aspirations or a goal-driven urgency pushing us from one activity to the next.

Belief in special creation provides a rationale for our existence. It bestows a purpose for life. The Westminster Catechism commences at this very point by asking: What is the chief end of man? To which it answers: "Man's chief end is to glorify God and to enjoy Him forever."

At the moment I'm working on manuscript revisions. Outside a torrential downpour is pounding against the windows. I'm reminded of those who enjoy watching old movies on rainy days. Topping my own list of all-time favorites is the 1959 blockbuster *Ben-Hur*, starring the late Charlton Heston as Judah Ben-Hur. The film's chariot race is one of Hollywood's greatest cinematic achievements. No computer-generated special effects are at work, only the heart-pounding thrill of genuine action. The thunderous scene portrays Judah Ben-Hur in mortal combat with his one-time friend turned nemesis, Messala, a Roman officer.

The plot of the film unfolds as Messala, in his

misguided ambition to achieve greater prominence in the Roman Empire, falsely accuses Judah, along with his mother and sister, of insurrection. The women are imprisoned while Judah is condemned to be a galley slave on a Roman warship. After three years of torturous labor chained to an oar, he's called to appear before the newly dispatched Roman Consul, Quintus Arrius.

The scene reveals Judah's belief that life has purpose and meaning despite his cruel betrayal.

He finds the commander asleep in his quarters. The Roman commander suddenly awakens. "Why are you here?"

Judah responds, "I was ordered to report to you during my relief. "

Arrius: "Oh, yes. I'd forgotten. You could have killed me as I lay there. You're a condemned man. Why didn't you?"

Judah: "I'm not ready to die."

Arrius: "What do you think will save you?"

Judah: "The God of my fathers. "

Arrius: "Your God has forsaken you. He has no more power than the images I pray to. My gods will not help me. Your God will not help you…"

The Roman commander offers Judah an opportunity to be trained as a gladiator. Judah quickly refuses claiming, "I will not be here forever."

Arrius responds: "No? What would you do if

> you escaped?"
>
> Judah: "Two people were condemned with me, my mother and sister, even though they were innocent. I will not rest..."
>
> Arrius: "You do not say that you were innocent."
>
> Judah: "Would it do any good to say it again?"
>
> Arrius: "No. But consider my offer carefully. You will never escape while we are victorious. If we are not, you will sink with this ship, chained to your oar."
>
> Judah: "I cannot believe that God has let me live these three years to die chained to an oar."
>
> Arrius: "It's a strange, stubborn faith you keep, to believe that existence has a purpose."

Much like Arrius, some are doubtful that "existence has a purpose." For those confined to such thinking hope embraces little more than what this hurried world can offer. In contrast, Ben-Hur's God-centered perspective meant life held a purpose—a reason for existence. His hope firmly embraced a spiritual reality, as should ours.

Following his great discovery of relativity, Einstein spent the last twenty years of his life devoted to the discovery of what he termed the Unified Field Theory. Attempting to prove electromagnetism and gravity were different manifestations of a single fundamental "field," he desperately sought a means to explain the nature and behavior of all matter and energy in the universe within a single equation. He never found his unifying factor. Neither has anyone else. It remains an ongoing mystery.

For those willing to look elsewhere however, there is a unifying force going largely unnoticed—most especially by the science community. This single source of power binds the entire universe together allowing natural laws to work in perfect harmony. This singular force is none other than the God of creation. While we dare not relegate our Creator to a "unified field" equation, the Scriptures reveal the Lord is, "upholding and maintaining and guiding and propelling the universe by His mighty word of power" (Heb.1:3 AMP). Identifying God as the power behind—and the reason for—our universe is a liberating thought.

THE PROBLEM OF PAIN

Many struggle to accept divine creation because of the pain and suffering that permeates our world. For the evolutionist these are simply the consequences—the natural order of things—in a world guided by random chance. Ironically, for those who do accept creation as the origin of life the same sticky problem remains. Why does a God of love allow pain and suffering? Moreover, why does He allow evil to exist and seemingly ignore our hardships, suffering, and prayers?

For those holding a worldview that excludes

the supernatural these questions ostensibly strengthen their argument. Admittedly, there are times when faith in God seemingly offers a less than satisfactory explanation for human atrocities, natural disasters, or random acts of violence. Entire books have been written addressing this issue of evil. Suffice it to say within our limited space, that much of the answer lies in a God who values our free will as a gift worthy of the risk of its consequences.

Why, beyond this reason, would God allow evil to persist through the centuries or specific hardships to disrupt individual lives remains for the present largely a mystery. Yet our inability to fully grasp God's methods, intentions, or sovereignty is not surprising. Can the finite creature expect to wholly grasp the infinite God? The Lord reveals this very fact when he reveals:

> *"For My thoughts are not your thoughts, Nor are your ways My ways, says the LORD. For as the heavens are higher than the earth, so are My ways higher than your ways, and My thoughts than your thoughts."* — Isaiah 55:8,9

We are reminded again of Job, a man overtaken by crushing affliction. Strangely, he was kept in the dark regarding the terrible ordeal he faced of loosing his health, his wealth, and his children. The Lord remained silent as Job wrestled for answers. God never revealed to Job why he faced such lamentable hardship. All along God's intention was to provide something of greater valuable than a quick answer upon which Job could rest his faith. Job was being led to keep his eyes focused solely upon the Lord for his consolation and to look beyond his immediate circumstances.

Where is the focus of your hope? Where do you find your consolation? Despite what some may feel, God's silence never indicates a lack of compassion or concern. In Job's case, that silence meant he was in the Lord's school of divine instruction. There he learned that spiritual truth sometimes surpasses our sensibilities.

> God's silence never indicates a lack of compassion or concern.

In the end Job came away with two valuable lessons. The same lessons we must take up in this world of hurt and hurry. First, Job learned to trust the Lord despite divine silence. Though unable to make sense of his tragic ordeal, Job came to understand God's purposes are not always in keeping with our own desires or feelings.

Secondly, Job learned to worship God for who He is, not for what He might do. The Lord himself must become the central focus of our love and devotion.

When hardships remain at the door we mistakenly perceive God's inaction to remove them as callous or uncaring. Nothing is further from the truth. God's very nature is one of care and concern. Admittedly He does not hesitate to occasionally use adversity as a means of driving us deeper into His arms. This was certainly true in Job's case.

The Lord's most valuable lessons are generally taught in the schoolroom of adversity. Unfortunately God's instruction is at times tied to obscurity. We might never know why we are suddenly faced with a tragedy. Why the layoff? Why the cancer? Why the children's rebellion? Why the shooting? Why the house fire? Why the betrayal of a friend? Much like us, Job never found out the reason for his string of personal tragedies. But Job's experience does teach us one thing that will help during our own difficulties. God's purposes, though not always revealed, nevertheless exist.

At first Job had his sights firmly fixed upon the Lord following his personal tragedy. His initial reaction was a firm proclamation of faith, "The LORD gave, and the LORD has taken away; Blessed be the name of the LORD" (Job 1:21). But calamity struck again. This time Job's health was the focus of attack. We applaud Job as he reprimands his wife, lashing out against her poor advice to "Curse God and die." He declares, "You speak as one of the foolish women speaks. Shall we indeed accept good from God, and shall we not accept adversity?" At this point Job's spiritual outlook remained intact.

But shortly thereafter we read that Job "opened his mouth and cursed the day of his birth." Clearly a dramatic transformation has taken place. In light of Job's earlier declaration of faith such a somber exclamation is puzzling. Why, we wonder, this extraordinary change of attitude? The answer is time.

Like the rest of us facing trials, Job expected some degree of timely relief from his anguish. It never came. While most of us can endure struggles on our own for a few days or weeks, when the realization finally hits that relief is not forthcoming our outlook on life often changes—and usually not for the better.

As a realist Job understood that virtue alone was no guarantee against trouble. He anticipated however that God would eventually reveal the reason for his afflictions. He assumed his righteous living owed him at least that much. When the expected explanation for his troubles failed to materialize Job fell to demanding a reason from God. With only silence in reply Job became a disheartened man. Much like us, Job was asking, "Why"? It's an all-to-common response to life's troubles. We easily relate to Job's anguish as he cries out,

> *"My soul loathes my life; I will give free course to my complaint, I will speak in the bitterness of my soul. I will say to God, 'Do not condemn me; Show me why You contend with me."* — Job 10:1,2

Eventually God confronts Job. It was not at all what he expected, but that divine intervention was exactly what Job needed. While Job's belief in God never wavered, his hope had withered and died. He saw no reason for his suffering. Moreover, the Lord seemed remote—inaccessible—unconcerned about his pains or pleas. Admit it, at times you have much in common with Job. God seems distant, unconcerned, and unresponsive to your prayers.

God's intervention came through a series of questions Job found impossible to answer. Yet the seed of hope's renewal sprouted during that encounter. Those questions allowed Job to catch sight of his limited understanding in light of God's infinite wisdom. He internalized the reality of divine sovereignty over the affairs of this world. Job refocused his hope upon the Lord and took his eyes off his

> Those questions allowed Job to catch sight of his own limited understanding...

devastating misfortunes. Though deprived of any explanation for his ordeal, Job humbly confesses, "I have uttered what I did not understand…" Satisfied with Job's renewed humility and newfound spiritual insight, God blesses him with restored health, renewed wealth, and ten new children.

The story of Job mirrors our own reaction to trouble. When the dark clouds of mystery shroud God's reasoning, we cry out for answers. We cannot help ourselves. We desperately seek some justification for our difficulties. Yet God is under no obligation to explain every reason for our trials and tribulations.

On the plus side however one thing is evident. Behind God's silence His purposes are constantly at work. If our hope is to live and thrive when faced with misfortune then the spiritual insight gained by Job must become our own.

True, God is silent at times but not altogether. He speaks openly by means of the Bible. Its pages graciously provide many solid answers to our earnest questions. It imparts spiritual insight and addresses many of our heartfelt concerns. Through the revelation of Scripture we learn suffering was foreign to God's original creation. The Bible details Adam's disobedience and the ensuing fall into sin that transformed a paradise for the living into a prison for the dying. This revelation alone answers much of the "w*hy*" for the suffering in this world.

Spiritual understanding fosters hope. Admittedly some difficulties remain. For instance, why some work hard and never get ahead while others prosper remains a mystery; or why some people are healed in answer to prayer while others remain ill is perplexing. Nevertheless, our lack of understanding does not limit our ability to have absolute assurance that God's purposes are decidedly being worked out.

Hope anchored to the unfailing Word of God far surpasses a skeptical "hope so" attitude that often renders life unpalatable. Living hope holds an assurance of God's abiding love regardless of circumstances or divine silence. A belief in the God of Scripture renders an awareness that the origin of life is altogether supernatural—not happenstance. Consequently, behind our existence lives a spiritual reality that bestows legitimate meaning to life.

※ ※ ※

KEY TRUTH #2 – Living Hope Rests upon the Foundation of Jesus Christ.

A faith that rests upon a flawed premise accomplishes little. Just ask Larry and Elmer.

While hunting one day these two friends managed to get lost deep in the woods. Trying to stay positive Larry said, "Don't worry. All we have to do is shoot into the air three times, stay where we are, and someone will find us."

That advice sounded good to Elmer so they shot three times into the air. They waited for a time, but no one came. They agreed to try it again; still no response.

They decided to give it one last try. "I hope it works this time," said Elmer. "We're down to our last three arrows."

Larry and Elmer were on the right track, but sadly their hope—their faith—was misguided. Maybe you recognize Larry or Elmer in the mirror. You rush through life knowing you must have faith in *something*, but you struggle to find an unyielding foundation upon which to build your hope in this hurried and often hurtful world.

Hope, in and of itself, neither eases troubled minds nor mends broken hearts. It's the object of our hope that fortifies the soul. The object, or foundation of our hope, must withstand the constant pressure we're under in our heroic effort to make ends meet, raise our children, or face unyielding difficulties. A hope ultimately tied to this tempestuous world often turns out like Larry and Elmer's silent arrow—a step in the right direction but unsupported by the facts.

Omar Khayyam, the 10th century Persian poet and philosopher, describes how fleeting a hope is when resting upon the wrong foundation:

> The worldly hope men set their hearts upon
> Turns to ash—or it prospers; and anon,
> Like snow upon the desert's dusty face
> Lighting a little hour or two—is gone.

In contrast William Barclay, one-time divinity professor at the University of Glasgow writes:

> When a man's hope is in God, it cannot turn to dust and ashes. When a man's hope is in God, it cannot be disappointed. When a man's hope is in the love of God, it can never be an illusion...God loves us with an everlasting love backed by an everlasting power.[21]

Let's face it; life's pace will never slow down.

Neither will we find immunity from all our woes. Out of necessity, the foundation of our hope must hold up under the weight of our struggles. A living hope rests upon that which is unaffected by the gale force winds of life's tumultuous storms or the brutal pace of modern life.

John Dewey put his finger on the pulse of our culture when he remarked, "Man lives in a world of surmise, of mystery, of uncertainties." Real hope cannot rest on uncertainties. By settling our hope on that which is unchanging, we gain relief from the stress of insecurity and the fear it fosters. God alone is the one constant in this ever-changing world. He alone is unchanging, and thus a solid foundation upon which to build our trust. He must be the object of our hope. Anything else is but trusting the shifting sands of wishful thinking and random chance.

> Out of necessity, the foundation of our hope must hold up under the weight of our struggles.

A living hope embraces more than an intellectual belief in God. It rests upon a personal relationship with the Father through faith in the sufficiency of the Son for our redemption. Jesus Himself calls attention to this truth when He declares:

> *"I am the way, the truth, and the life;*
> *no man comes to the Father except by me."*
> — John 14:6

Living hope is rooted in the living Lord. And the resurrection of Jesus Christ is proof that the Lord lives and now sits on the right hand of the Father

Jesus is the constant in a constantly changing world. Hebrews 13:8 makes this bold proclamation, *"Jesus Christ is the same yesterday, today, and forever."* Jesus is unchangeable, making Him the obvious choice upon which to rest our hope and build our lives.

> *"No other foundation can anyone lay than that which is laid, which is Jesus Christ".*
> — 1Cor. 3:11

In Jesus Christ we'll find the genuine serenity we seek for in this hurried and hurting world of ours. God's promises of strength, security, peace, and provision are freely at the disposal of those who place their trust in Christ.

More significantly a second advantage comes with trusting in Christ. Through Him is the opportunity to inherit, not only abundant life in the here and now, but also eternal life in the hereafter.

The sufficiency for this salvation comes by way of Christ's sacrifice on our behalf. The price for our redemption was paid in full at the cross over 2,000 years ago. Our heavenly Father offers this gift of salvation through the merits of His Son. It is ours for the asking. Only the willingness to accept the gift by simple faith remains.

The Bible assures us that salvation comes by means of simple faith:

> *"For by grace you have been saved through faith, and that not of yourselves; it is the gift of God, not as a result of works, so that no one may boast."* — Eph. 2:8 (NASV)

Charles Simeon (1759-1836) sorts out this truth that hope in Christ, and not our efforts, leads to salvation. He writes:

> We must not think our hope well-founded, unless it produce in us the fruits of righteousness, yet we must not imagine that our righteousness is to be the ground of our hope, or even our warrant to hope in Christ. The only ground of our hope must be found in Christ, and in the promises, which God has made to those who believe in him. We must go to Christ as sinners; and then he will enable us to live as saints. This distinction is clearly marked in the test: our hope in Christ is to precede, not to follow, the purification of our hearts: and our holiness is to be the fruit, not the root, of our hope.

Living hope is built upon a foundation that is not tethered to this world. It's a hope that unlocks the eternality of the soul and glimpses God in all His glory, majesty, and holiness; a God of love and compassion who desires to be our sufficiency for peace and joy and the source of our salvation for the world to come.

David Livingston, famed 19th century explorer and missionary, had long held that his successful exploits in Africa were due to the sufficiency of God. His journal resides in the British Museum where, in reference to Christ's promise, "I am with you always even unto the end of the age."[22] Livingston wrote, "It is the word of a gentleman of the strictest and most sacred honor, and there's an end of it."

This same full measure of assurance held by Livingston is still available for those willing to stand upon the flawless foundation of Jesus Christ and receive Him into their hearts and lives.

✼ ✼ ✼

KEY TRUTH #3: Living Hope Comes by Placing our Lives into the Hands of an All-knowing and Merciful God.

Ironically, despite God's ample qualifications to offer peace and happiness, we defiantly struggle against surrendering to His control. The reason for this is simple. We firmly believe self-determination is the avenue to happiness. Our innate desire is to manage the direction of our own lives. We find a sense of security in keeping a firm grip on the wheel as we steer down life's highway.

Some years back a popular bumper sticker read: *God is my Co-pilot*. Though few would argue the merits of God as a co-pilot, most are reluctant to actually allow Him in the pilot's seat. For many, the idea of allowing God to steer the direction of their lives is unthinkable. We resist surrender fearing He will take us in the wrong direction. We dread the thought of our plans and lives disappearing in the rearview mirror.

Loosing control can be a frightening prospect, but our concerns are unfounded. God desires to bless us with His grace, mercy, and love as we travel down the road of crushing schedules, failed expectations, or those detours of His choosing.

Of course, from God's perspective there are no "wrong" roads. Every turn, every bend, every detour is meant to lead us directly to a genuine hope in the living Lord. Chronic worry, emotional overloads, and frayed nerves, all point to our tenacious grip on life's steering wheel. The solution as someone once observed is to, "Let go, and let God."

I caught sight of a second bumper sticker several months later that underscores this truth. It read: *If God is your co-pilot change seats!*

A subtle transformation takes place when we yield to God's direction. What we initially imagine as a less desirable route surprisingly turns out to be the road of greater blessings. We discover the Lord has abundantly supplied our every need, addressed our every concern, and calmed our anxious hearts. Joy and peace now become our fellow passengers in this new direction in life.

English statesman Oliver Cromwell (1599–1658) once left England for the European continent on national business. It was customary at the time for his valet to share the same room. That night Cromwell tossed and turned being unable to sleep, while his servant slept soundly. Cromwell woke the man up and confessed he was worried something would go wrong during his meeting with national leaders that following day.

"Master," asked the valet. "Did God rule the world before we were born?"

"Most assuredly."

"And will he rule the world after we are dead?"

"Certainly He will."

"Then, Master, I suggest we let Him rule in the present as well."

That's sound advice for any of us. There's great wisdom in trusting the One who knows and holds the future. Tomorrow is hidden from us. What lies around the next bend remains a mystery. An unknown detour may loom ahead, frustrating our plans or forcing us onto a less desirable road in life. In spite of such possibilities, biblical hope remains fixed upon the Lord with a firm belief that all of life's circumstances, whatever they turn out to be, work together for the spiritual benefit of His children. The apostle Paul underscores this truth when he writes:

> *"...All things work together for good to them who love God, to those who are called according to His purpose."* — Romans 8:28

Trusting God is the life's blood of a dynamic,

living hope. Two vital elements fortify our hope in the living Lord.

- **COURAGE** – Courage stems from a deep trust in God. When fear strikes or problems arise beyond our limited ability to resolve them we need a hefty dose of courage. Hope without courage is anemic. Its remedy is a booster shot of trusting the integrity of God and His Word. Spiritual courage is believing God means what He says.

    Israel's exodus from slavery is a classic example of needed courage. With the Egyptian army advancing from behind and the Red Sea blocking their escape ahead, the Israelites were instructed by Moses to, "Stand still, and see the salvation of the Lord."

    Their instinct was to run; somewhere—anywhere; but the people stood still and one of history's greatest miracles took place: the parting of the Red Sea.

    Caught between the Egyptian army and the Red Sea, the Israelites faced a life-threatening situation with no avenue of escape. Their deliverance lay beyond their ability, but they were not beyond God's ability. The only condition was to trust and obey the Lord's command to "stand still." Courage was the obvious need of the hour.

Trapped by our own fear of facing an unknown future there are times when God desires for us to "stand still," affording Him the chance to perform a miracle in our lives. Those insurmountable trials we face are God's opportunity to show Himself strong on our behalf. It's once been said, "Whatever enlarges hope will also exalt courage."

Those with a stalwart hope in God are unstoppable. Their courage smothers fear, replacing it with a deep-rooted sense of trust in the Lord. Need a shot of courage? Open the hope chest of Scripture. You'll find the courage you need by settling your faith upon God's promises and relying upon His good and gracious character.

- Courage is characteristic of those who know God - Daniel 11:32.
- "Be of good courage, and he shall strengthen your heart, all ye that hope in the LORD" - Psalm 31:24.

- **CONFIDENCE** – Besides courage, living hope possesses a deep confidence in God. Such confidence takes root when that in which we place our hope has been tried and tested and subsequently found both effective and reliable. Of all the world's possibilities only God, having been tried and tested at every turn of the human experience, consistently proves Himself capable of meeting the deepest needs of the human heart.

Our confidence in the Lord is further strengthened in considering His attributes. To begin with, God is omnipotent. Nothing is beyond His ability or power. Meaning He has the ability to change any situation.

As a virgin, Mary questioned how she could possibly give birth to the Christ-child. The angel who brought her the startling news simply said, "Is anything too hard for the Lord?" The answer of course is, "No." Nothing this world throws at us is beyond God's remedy. He is able to "move mountains" on our behalf should He choose to do so. Whatever life dishes out, God has the power to change it (or us!), improve it, or eliminate it.

Our confidence also finds a boost in considering God's omniscience. The Lord is all knowing. His infinite knowledge includes knowing us intimately and knowing every circumstance of our lives. Neither our troubles nor our concerns escape His notice. Just as He's aware of every sparrow that falls (Luke 12:6), so too is the Lord aware of every weight we carry, every struggle we face, and every adversity this hurried world throws into our laps.

Bolstering our confidence still further is God's omnipresence. Thus, no road we travel is beyond His reach. No circumstance we encounter lies outside His abiding presence. His children are never abandoned. In both the storms of life and the rat race of tomorrow, God's presence is available to comfort, support, and guide.

We cannot leave off without briefly considering God's dependability. The consistency of each sunrise; the endless progression of the seasons; the endless water cycle; the unvaried laws of nature; the fidelity of planetary motion all illustrate God's dependability. His reliability thunders from the mountain peaks echoing into the hearts of those willing to listen. Just as we encounter God's faithfulness in nature, He is faithful to strengthen, support, and supply our every need when we are drained by a world that never slows down. Reliability and dependability are the hallmarks of God's character. How then can we fail to have confidence in His watch care?

- Confidence is characteristic of believing God's Word - I Timothy 1:12.
- God working in and through our lives brings confidence - Philippians 1:6.

The Lord's concern for His people is demonstrated at every turn in the Bible. When Israel wandered from the Lord's guidance He reminded them:

> *'For I know the plans I have for you', declares the LORD, 'plans for welfare and not for*

calamity to give you a future and a hope.

'Then you will call upon Me and come and pray to Me, and I will listen to you.

'You will seek Me and find Me when you search for Me with all your heart.'

— Jeremiah 29:11-13 (NASV)

Burdens overwhelming? Is life's load too heavy? Rat race running you ragged? Call upon the One who replaces panic with peace and hurry with happiness. Place your confidence in Him. Step out by courageous faith and invite the Lord to pilot the direction of your life. At the same time call upon the Lord who provides salvation for the repentant soul when life's journey has ended. For those who rush through life without a thought of eternity, God makes a simple and straightforward offer:

"That if you confess with your mouth the Lord Jesus and believe in your heart that God has raised Him from the dead, you will be saved. For with the heart one believes unto righteousness, and with the mouth confession is made unto salvation...for whoever calls upon the name of the Lord shall be saved."

—Romans 10:9,10,13

The water of God's Word quenches our thirst for answers. The Lord's abundant supply of living water from the Bible pours like Niagara into the precipice below—washing away all doubt, fear, and uncertainty.

There is a great confidence and peace in knowing the Lord's concern for our physical, emotional, and spiritual wellbeing is clearly demonstrated by the sacrifice of His Son. There is no doubt God loves His own, and He is more than able to provide for their every care.

Tension, stress, and anxiety are common ailments in today's harried world, resulting from life's unrelenting pressures. Pressures that can come through a family crisis, financial hardship, or our effort to keep pace with a world that fails to give us a moment's relief.

The remedy? Call upon Him. He will answer your plea for peace in this world and your cry for salvation in the world to come. Remember, our trust—our hope—in the Lord is rooted in His gracious character. The Lord's promise to Jeremiah is no less true today then when first given:

> Our trust—our hope—in the Lord is rooted in His gracious character.

"Call to me, and I will answer you, and show you great and mighty things, which you do not know."
—Jeremiah 33:3

A God of Love

> "He who does not love
> does not know God; for God is love."
> — I John 4:8

Love and holiness are the very essence of God's character. While a number of other attributes are ascribed to God in the Bible, love and holiness stand out foremost. Regrettably the full bearing of God's character is often lost to our pre-conceived notions of love.

Few would deny that the word "love" has experienced cultural assassination over the years. Our understanding of true love has been distorted by the downward slide of societal norms. The significance of the word has been all but lost through sexual promiscuity and comedic television portrayals. Love has been largely redefined as infatuation or sexual attraction. America's high divorce rate further exemplifies that "love" for many is merely a temporary commitment. Such a demeaning direction muddies the water when defining God's love.

Simply put, God's love is sacrificial. Providing what's needed for our benefit is His very nature. Jesus spelled this out with regard to our need for salvation. When approached by the religious leader Nicodemus one night Jesus revealed that, "God so loved the world He *gave* His only begotten Son..."[23] In seeing our spiritual need for a restored relationship with Him, the Father willingly gave His Son as the payment for our sin.

J.I. Packer rightly describes God's love by pointing directly to the cross and the substitutionary death of Jesus Christ on our behalf:

> The measure of love is how much it gives, and the measure of the love of God is the gift of His only Son to be made man, and to die for sins, and so to become the one mediator who can bring us to God...The New Testament writers constantly point to the Cross of Christ as the crowning proof of the reality and boundlessness of God's love. Thus, John goes straight on from his initial statement that 'God is love' to say, 'In this was manifested the love of God towards us, because that God sent his only begotten Son into the world, that we might have life through Him. Herein is love, not that we loved God, but that he loved us, and sent his Son to be the propitiation for our sins.[24]

To be sure, God's love offers more than a way to the soul's salvation. With a broad sweep of compassion God's love embraces the practical. It generously provides for our daily needs and ignites His concern for our difficulties.

Often quoted at weddings, first Corinthians

chapter thirteen in the Bible defines the very qualities that make up the essence of love. It reveals that love...

> "...Rejoices in the truth; bears all things, believes all things, hopes all things, endures all things. Love never fails...And now abide faith, hope, love, these three; but the greatest of these is love."

Our difficulty is fully grasping such love—especially one that "never fails." Yet God carries this unfailing love for His children. His love is unconditional, unquenchable, and unfathomable.

Again Packer makes the point:

> What matters supremely, therefore, is not, in the last analysis, the fact that I know God, but that larger fact which underlies it—the fact that *He knows me.* I am graven on the palms of His hands. I am never out of His mind...He knows me as a friend, one who loves me; and there is no moment when His eye is off me, or His attention distracted from me, and no moment, therefore, when His care falters...This is momentous knowledge. There is unspeakable comfort...in knowing that God is constantly taking knowledge of me in love and watching over me for my good.
>
> There is tremendous relief in knowing that His love to me is utterly realistic, based at every point on prior knowledge of the worst about me, so that no discovery now can disillusion him about me, in the way I am so

often disillusioned about myself...[25]

God's loving compassion draws us to Himself. His desire is to see us through our heartaches, pressing schedules, family pains, and financial woes. His unfailing love sustains our courage in the face of adversity. Mark it down—nothing separates the believer from the love of God.

> *"...in all these things we are more than conquerors through Him who loved us. For I am persuaded that neither death nor life, nor angels nor principalities nor power, nor things present nor things to come, nor height nor depth, nor any other created thing, shall be able to separate us from the love of God which in Christ Jesus our Lord."* — Romans 8:37-39

Turn on the nightly news, read the newspapers, search the Internet—all testify that the gale-force winds of our rushed world are driving us madly across life's tumultuous sea. The question is, where does our hope lie? How we answer that question sets our sails and determines our course.

Centuries ago the southern tip of Africa was called the "Cape of Tempests." Its tumultuous seas and frequent hostile weather caused even sea-hardened sailors to fear passage through the hazardous waterway. Many lost their lives in the attempt.

In August 1486, the Portuguese navigator Bartholomeu Dias set sail to find a trade route to

Asia around the southern point of Africa. While on his voyage a fierce storm erupted, forcing his ships off course into what is now known as Mossel Bay. Dias then realized he had already passed the tip of Africa and had actually discovered the sea route to the East. On his return voyage Dias changed the name "Cape of Tempests" to Cabo da boa Esperanza, "Cape of Good Hope."

How foolish to hoist our sails and tack into the winds of uncertainty in this world. Our ship of *Circumstantial Hope* is easily stranded upon the jagged shoals of life's stormy seas by the winds of misfortune. Gale-driven waves of despair crash over her decks. A thick fog of apprehension and fear hides the Lord from view. Confined to *Circumstantial Hope* we are unable to discern the Lord's good intention to steer us safely to distant shores. In the midst of the rat race we are too preoccupied to sense His concern for our welfare. And yet, His deepest desire is to Captain our ship.

We sail through many storms on life's journey. Yet no matter their fury they cannot suppress the inner peace and hope we possess when Christ pilots our ship and becomes the Captain of our soul. Jesus knows every aspect of life's perilous seas. He's familiar with life's strong currents, its hidden shoals, and the shallow reefs that threaten to dash our hope upon rocky shores.

Set your heart upon Christ and come aboard His ship, *Tranquility*. With Christ at the helm hope thrives. We can rest assured He will successfully navigate our lives through the treacherous tempests around the "Cape of Good Hope." Better still, with our Captain at the helm we will one day sail beyond the horizon of our worldly existence into the far-reaching eternal day.

God's invitation is for all to take passage upon His ship *Tranquility*. Hoist the sails of faith and call upon the name of the Lord Jesus to find peace in the world now and salvation in the world to come.

Surrender the helm of your hurried life to the One who is best suited to Captain your soul. Let Him be your *Hope...in a Hurried* World. All that remains now is to tack into the wind by faith where God promises His children,

> *"I will never leave you, nor forsake you"*
> ~ Hebrews 13:5 ~

> Heaven was his hope,
> and Providence his guide.
> *Alton Churchyard,
> Staffordshire*

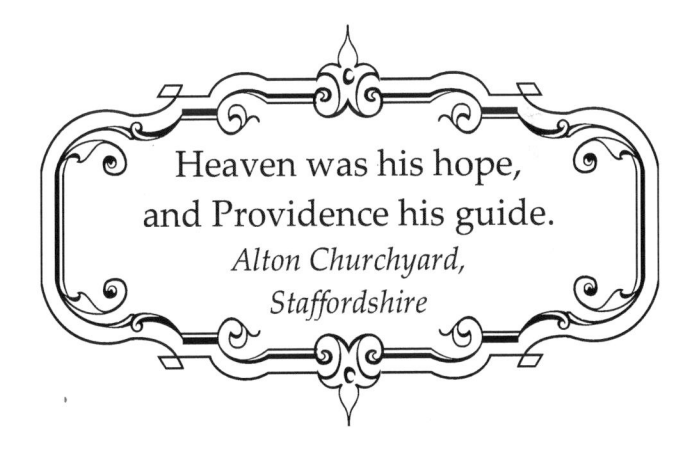

Acknowledgements

[1] Stephen Covey, A Roger Merrill, Rebecca R. Merrill. "First Things First: To Live, to Love, To Learn, to Leave a Legacy." (Simon & Schuster, 1994).

[2] Randy C. Alcorn, *Money Possessions and Eternity*, Tyndale House Publishers, Inc. Carol Stream, Illinois, ©2003, pg. 48

[3] Charles R. Swindoll, *Growing Strong in the Seasons of Life*, Multnomah Press, Portland, Oregon © 1983, Pg. 270.

[4] Arthur W. Pink, *The Seven Sayings of the Saviour on the Cross*, Baker Book House, Grand Rapids, Michigan, © 2006, pg. 104

[5] Larry Burkett, *What Ever Happened to the American Dream*, Moody Press, Chicago, Illinois © 1993

[6] J.I.Packer, *Knowing God*, InterVarsity Press, Downers Grove, Illinois,©1973; pgs.14,15

[7] Charles R. Swindoll, *Living on the Ragged Edge*, pg. 25; Word Books, Waco, Texas © 1985

[8] People Magazine, November 2008

[9] Ecclesiastes 12:1

[10] Ecclesiastes 12:3

[11] Elisabeth Elliot, *Keep A Quiet* Heart, Baker Book House, Grand Rapids, Michigan, © 2004

[12] Randy Alcorn, *Heaven*, Tyndale House Publishers, Inc., Carol Stream, Illinois, © 2004 by Eternal Perspective Ministries.

[13] John MacArthur, Senior pastor of Grace Community Church, California. Quoted by author's direct permission, 2010

[14] Warren W. Wiersbe, *The Bumps Are What You Climb On*, Baker Book House, Grand Rapids, Michigan, © 1980. pgs. 88,89

[15] Josh McDowell; *The New Evidence that Demands a Verdict*; Thomas Nelson Publishers, Nashville, TN ©1999; pg. 593

[16] John Blanchard; *Is Anybody Out There?*; Evangelical Press, Faverdale North, Darlington, England © 2006; pg. 12

[17] Ibid; pg. 244

[18] Francis A. Schaeffer, *The Complete Works of Francis A. Schaeffer, Volume One, A Christian View of Philosophy and Culture*, Crossway Books, 1300 Crescent Street, Wheaton, Ill. 60187, © 1985, pg.45

[20] Raymond McHenry; *Something to Think About*, Hendrickson Publishers, Peabody, MA, © 1998, pg. 204

[20] Henry M. Morris, *Men of Science, Men of God*, Master Books, P.O. Box 1606, El Cajon, CA 92022, © 1982,1988, pg. 85

[21] William Barclay, *The Letter to the Romans (Revised Edition)*, The Westminster Press, Philadelphia, PA © 1975, pg 75

[22] Matthew 28:20

[23] John 3:16

[24] J.I.Packer, *Knowing God*, InterVarsity Press, Downers Grove, Illinois, ©1973; pg.114 / I John 4:9ff

[25] Ibid; pg.37

Made in the USA
Columbia, SC
26 August 2017